DO.BE.ISMs

DOUBLISMs

DO.BE.ISMs

Reflections On The Twelve Steps And The Gifts of Sobriety

D.B. and Doc

 iUniverse

DO.BE.ISMS
REFLECTIONS ON THE TWELVE STEPS
AND THE GIFTS OF SOBRIETY

iUniverse books may be ordered through booksellers or by contacting:

iUniverse LLC
1663 Liberty Drive
Bloomington, IN 47403
www.iuniverse.com
1-800-Authors (1-800-288-4677)

Because of the dynamic nature of the Internet, any web addresses or
links contained in this book may have changed since publication and
may no longer be valid. The views expressed in this work are solely those
of the author and do not necessarily reflect the views of the publisher,
and the publisher hereby disclaims any responsibility for them.

Any people depicted in stock imagery provided by Thinkstock are
models, and such images are being used for illustrative purposes only.
Certain stock imagery © Thinkstock.

ISBN: 978-1-4917-3842-9 (sc)
ISBN: 978-1-4917-3843-6 (e)

Library of Congress Control Number: 2014910954

Printed in the United States of America.

iUniverse rev. date: 08/13/2014

Dedicated to our Higher Power, the program of
Alcoholics Anonymous, and all of you in recovery.

CONTENTS

FOREWORD

This book tells the story of two individuals, D.B. and Doc who met through a meeting of Alcoholics Anonymous. The two of them were inspired to write Do.Be.Isms, which is intended to be a commentary on the Twelve Steps that make up the AA program. During the book, you will be "sitting in" on a series of meetings between the two as D.B. attempts to be an encouragement to Doc, while helping him understand the rewards available to a person willing to commit to every aspect of the Twelve Steps.

D.B.'s own commitment eventually inspires Doc to acknowledge and accept the principles of Alcoholics Anonymous, along with believing that the Higher Power of his understanding can do for him those things he could not do himself. D.B. and Doc were both on the road to ruin in their personal lives because of alcohol, and now they have found a new path. Although this new path is not without its challenges or aches and pains, it is filled with fellow travelers along with beautiful sights and scenes. There are no dead ends, only detours. With fellow journeyers consisting of men and women from all races, creeds, and backgrounds, we get to laugh and cry, to identify and celebrate, to give and receive and love.

At one point D.B. and Doc both had a falling out. Doc never thought he had it within him to give up his resentments and forgive, but he eventually does. Thus a new journey was born: this one, this book.

While Doc likes to analyze each idea in-depth, D.B. prefers to keep things simple, and he does so with one-liners that seem to capture some critical element of each of the Twelve Steps.

We know that we could never give true justice to the brilliance and depth of the Twelve Steps, but this book is our attempt to give back some of what we have found. We have learned that there is always more treasure to mine from the steps. This book provides questions at the end of each chapter for you to consider as part of your inquiry into sobriety and spirituality. It is our hope and prayer that this book will be of particular help to the newcomer.

The Twelve Steps and brief excerpts from Alcoholics Anonymousare reprinted with permission of Alcoholics Anonymous World Services, Inc. (AAWS). Permission to reprint the Steps and Traditions is not intended to imply that AAWS has reviewed or approved the contents of this publication, or that A.A. necessarily agrees with the views expressed herein. A.A. is a program of recovery from alcoholism only—use of the Steps and Traditions in connection with programs and activities which are patterned after A.A., but which address other problems, or in any other non-A.A. context, does not imply otherwise.

ACKNOWLEDGMENTS

This book would not have been possible without our Higher Power, Alcoholics Anonymous founders, Bill W., and Dr. Bob, and those countless others who came before and touched lives, one life at a time. The late Bill W. and Dr. Bob were two ordinary people with extraordinary problems. They could not stop drinking and they could not stop thinking about stopping. The more they tried to fix the problem on their own, the bigger it became. It is hard to know why it took so many years for Alcoholics Anonymous to be born, or why God waited so long to orchestrate events to unfold the way they have. Surely, we are the beneficiaries of now having a solution to a problem that causes destruction and death, physically, psychologically, and spiritually.

Alcohol is a chemical and we as humans—just like everything in this world—are made of up chemicals, atoms combined into molecules, which are combined into compounds, which in turn combine to form the stuff of life. Somehow, those inanimate physical entities give rise to something that is not physical, and that is us, you, the "I Am." The "I Am" is what makes you, YOU. It is the whisper of your own inner voice, your SOUL. How a chemical called alcohol can affect the soul, sometimes slowly, and sometimes quickly, is really a mystery, although science continues to uncover more and more about the biological processes involved. For some of us—and if you are one of us—this book is for you; over time, the chemical called alcohol, can eat away at the body, and destroy the soul, the "I Am."

This book is written by two individuals, D.B. and Doc. We are people who likely would not have met but for our common problem and common solution. We are indebted to the program of Alcoholics Anonymous, and the people who have given us permission to make brief references to The Big Book of Alcoholics Anonymous and the Twelve Steps. We emphasize that we are not experts and any and all comments made in reference to The Big Book and the Twelve Steps are our opinions only, and are not endorsed by Alcoholics Anonymous or any organization. Just like you, we are grateful to have found a solution, and one day at a time, hope to work the steps in a way that we best understand. We are thankful to our parents, of blessed memory, our spouses, and all of those who came before us and who have shone a light on our path.

We are grateful to our Higher Power, who has given us a new lease on life and restored our souls.

INTRODUCTION

This book, DO.BE.ISMs, is intended to be helpful to those who are on a journey for not only physical sobriety, but also emotional sobriety which provides a measure of peace of mind and the feeling that we are right inside our own skin. The Big Book of Alcoholics Anonymous promises a new freedom and a new happiness, provided we are willing to follow a few simple steps: find a sponsor, work the steps, and go to meetings. This process, which we do one day at a time, is not always easy, but it does offer us something that we were always looking for: a purpose for our lives, and a connection to a source of Power that is real and loving. If you are like us, you have already sought the easier and softer way, with and without alcohol.

It seems that while we were able to obtain a temporary relief by getting a transient buzz or high, we were always left with something missing. Just as the feeling of alcohol gave us an elusive feeling that only works for a while, we could not shake the feeling that there was always something more, and in the rush to attain it we discovered that instead, we were left with a feeling of less and less inside.

We were inspired to write a book that provides an expression of our own souls and in doing so, touch yours.

If you find what you like, use it, and feel free to discard the rest. We are of the belief that there is no such thing as a coincidence, and what some people believe to be coincidences is simply God's way of remaining anonymous. We do not pretend we know who or are what God is, however we do have faith in a Higher Power who can and will heal our mind, body, and soul, while giving us a glimpse of heaven on earth.

Please feel free to substitute another word for "God" if that works for you. Please be aware that when we use the word "God" throughout this book we are referring to that which you regard as your Higher Power, and that force or power which will bring you strength, happiness, and blessing. Neither D.B. nor Doc has had any supernatural experiences, and thankfully, we have not heard voices or seen things that were not real. However, along with the normal feelings of frustration, worry, and feelings of restlessness, irritability and discontent, we have also experienced moments of something that was very precious and enduring: an attitude of gratitude.

Doc could not shake the feeling that D.B. had something that he wanted: a true conviction and faith that a Higher Power really existed and that this power could and would alter the fabric of our lives, but only if we did our part. While D.B. had this faith, Doc wasn't quite as sure and wanted to see the burning bush, but to date he still hasn't. One evening, in his anxious despair, at a time when he was not even thinking about alcohol, the idea came to Doc that he had to be around honest people. At the time, Doc did not think he had an alcohol problem, so why he would travel 50 kilometers away from his home to a meeting of Alcoholics Anonymous (he was embarrassed to be seen by anyone) still baffles him.

We believe that your Higher Power, whatever that is for you, can work miracles in your life. This book provides some commentary on the Twelve Steps, one of perhaps many ways to have a spiritual awakening in your life, which is a miracle of sorts. A spiritual awakening is, as The Big Book notes, a profound alteration in your reaction to life. It is a different future from the one you were going to have, one more aligned with who you were meant to be. It is a today that, although distinct from your past, is nevertheless informed by it.

It is a today that is not without its struggles and its demands or its upsets and thwarted intentions, but rather a today that provides you with the tools for staying strong and courageous, for moving toward your goals, as opposed to moving away from them; a today that offers inspiration, hope, and faith. It is a today with others, knowing that you are no longer alone.

Doc did see in D.B. the embodiment of a working Power that offered a new way of thinking, a new way of doing, and a new way of being. This is why the book is entitled: Do.Be.ISMs. Doc learned from D.B. that you cannot be something that you are not, and what you do both reflects and shapes who you are. As The Big Book says, we cannot give something we don't have. That truth is what really got to Doc. How do we have a spiritual awakening, some alteration in the way we see the world, and experience ourselves and others? D.B. didn't quite say it like this, but his whole demeanor, what he says and how he says it, revealed to me that my Higher Power will only do for me that which I cannot do for myself, and similarly this Higher Power will not do for me what I can do for myself. The sponsorship, the meetings, and the steps are the vehicles for tapping into and connecting with this Higher Power, as well as identifying and doing the next right thing. The miracle will eventually happen, so please do not leave before it does: a new way of thinking, doing, and being.

The clouds may come and go, and tears of sadness fall, but the smiles will be brighter, the eyes more alive, and the soul more true to itself.

D.B. reminded Doc that you cannot rest on your laurels, that you cannot plant corn and pick pears, that although you can look back, you cannot go back, and that there is so little time and so much to love. Doc was always amused and smiled at the way D.B. packed a punch in order to reveal a particular principle. D.B. sometimes spoke in parables and Doc doesn't always really understand what D.B. is saying. D.B. had a stroke and its effects, combined with his alcoholism, affected his memory and verbal fluency, which sometimes makes it difficult for Doc to understand him. Doc recognizes though that D.B.'s spirit has come alive and that his soul, his "I Am," has found the answers to its prayers. Doc knows that D.B. has something of value to impart, and he does so with what Doc calls "Do.Be.ISMs."

The "Ism" of the book stands for the memorable one-liners that D.B. offers, but it is also an acronym for "I, self, and me." These one- liners enable us to reach for a vision that is greater than ourselves.

Doc's sponsor, Les, says that the "Ism" also stands for "incredibly short memory." That is, alcoholics have an incredibly short memory regarding the negative outcomes that have come about as a result of their drinking, as well as their promises to their Higher Power who has provided grace and a new lease on life. We alcoholics have the tendency to default to being selfish and self-centered, unless we work the steps. The "I, self, me" narrows the scope of vision and leads to a self-centeredness that cuts us off from the sunlight of the spirit.

Who are you and what is your spirit? The following parable, which comes from an old Indian legend helps to illustrate this point.

An old Cherokee was teaching his grandson about life. "A fight is going on inside me," he said to the boy.

"It is a terrible fight and it is between two wolves. One wolf is evil – he is anger, envy, sorrow, regret, greed, arrogance, self-pity, guilt, resentment, inferiority, lies, false pride, superiority, and ego."

He continued, "The other wolf is good – he is joy, peace, love, hope, serenity, humility, kindness, benevolence, empathy, generosity, truth, compassion, and faith. The same fight is going on inside you – and inside every other person, too."

The grandson thought about the words he had just heard for a minute and then asked his grandfather, "Which wolf will win?"

The old Cherokee simply replied, "The one you feed the most."

As D.B. says . . . sometimes with a smile, sometimes with a frown, but always with conviction: "The choice is yours."

DO.BE.ISMs

1. You can run, you can hide, you can cover, but you can't get away
2. You can't change your disease but you can overcome it
3. There is one original; the rest is carbon copy
4. To win the race you've got to win you first
5. It's not what you eat; it's what's eating you
6. So little time, so much to love
7. You can't plant corn and pick pears
8. Speak victory, not defeat
9. The journey is long, the time is short
10. You can look back, but but don't go back
11. Time is not a commodity; time is a gift
12. Celebration is good but support is better

What are Do.Be.Isms?

"Do.Be.Isms" are power-packed one-liners that D.B. uses in his own way in order to capture the essence of each of the steps of Alcoholics Anonymous. These one-liners are our interpretation, and admittedly sometimes it is a stretch to link each "Do.Be.Ism" to one of the Twelve Steps, but we think it has some merit and for sure, the "Do.Be.Ism" has certainly helped the two of us. For those of you in the program, you undoubtedly have your own words, phrases, and interpretations of the steps; however, we humbly offer our interpretations in the hope that they might offer some value to you. Besides, when you become sober, the mind becomes more creative, and this book reflects our gratitude for the ability to be creative and inspired.

We both believe there are many paths to peace and serenity, which leads to the discovery of one's own truth and essence. The twelve-step plan involves the heart, the mind, and the soul. If you are like Doc, you may be initially perplexed and puzzled by the "Do.Be.Ism." It takes an effort to understand others, just like it also does for others to understand us on occasion.

Doc has eagerly and hungrily sought out answers from D.B. about how to work the steps, and what each one means. Doc insists on picking apart and analyzing each element of the steps. D.B. says this is okay but emphasizes the process is a simple program for complex people. D.B. is happy because he no longer has to take a drink. Everything else, he says, is a bonus. Not so for Doc. For him, while putting down the drink is a great and necessary step for basic survival, it is only the first in the hope of something more to come.

D.B. acknowledges that while there is always more to come, it is more important to know where you have come from.

An Attitude of Gratitude

He is talking about gratitude, and coming from a place of gratitude.

The essence of love is gratitude, and the essence of gratitude is love.

Love and gratitude are both feelings and actions. Going to meetings, working the steps with our sponsor, and prayer are the means of coping with the fury of all those forces that attempt to pull us away from gratitude and love. Remember, D.B. says life is a challenge, and just because you do not drink does not mean your life will not be like a roller coaster. At least with the Twelve Step program, you will feel like you are riding in the car as opposed to lying helpless on the tracks. It may be hard to feel love and gratitude when you are in the pit of despair, and if you are reading this you know what the pit of despair looks and feels like. There is a way out of the pit. You are no longer alone and the program promises you will experience a new freedom, so don't leave until the miracle happens.

The miracle manifests itself differently for each individual.

For D.B., the miracle is being free of the obsession to drink. For Doc, it is the sense that he can be comfortable inside of his own skin.

For others, it is restoring broken relationships or finding the career for which they are best suited, or realizing that they don't have to compare themselves to others to be happy. What would be a miracle for you?

Each "Do.Be.Ism" corresponds to one of the Twelve Steps and each of the steps corresponds to a principle. By working the steps, and with the grace of a Higher Power of your understanding, you will experience the spiritual joy of having an attitude of gratitude.

The Real You, Not the Fake You

One final point: as you read, discover the "I Am" that is doing the reading, the real you, not some fake version. The fake version of you is the one that drank. The drink was but a symptom of some other cause and condition. For Doc and D.B., the drink was a solution to a problem, and that solution then became the problem. They did not know that then but they know it now. It is interesting how one can be blindsided, caught off guard, and arrive at a destination they had no intention of visiting. As the saying goes, however, "The truth shall set you free."

In doing the steps, you will be set free. Along the way D.B. and Doc discovered that they were dishonest and fakes, full of shame, guilt and remorse. They felt trapped with no way out. They had hit bottom. You know when you have hit bottom: when you stop digging. Still, there are those among us who keep picking up the shovel. We have been there too. What we say is not as important as what we do. What we do, well, we all do it one day at a time. Our sobriety is done one day at a time, and it depends on our spiritual condition that day and not some other day. As D.B. says, "You can run but you cannot hide."

The Answer is "Yes"

Just like their sponsors who came before them, we were told that we were not special and unique, that others also suffer from negative and turbulent emotions and thoughts. Our sponsors told us that that they too were selfish, self-centered, and hurtful to others, but if we wanted it badly enough there was a way to be strengthened and healed. That is, if the "I AM" wants it badly enough. The Big Book promises us healing and a new way of life if that is what we truly sought and prayed for from our Higher Power, even if it is the God of our not understanding, as a fellow member with more than 60 years of sobriety has humbly said.

Impossible, you say. How can that be done, and can it really happen for me? The answer is "Yes," it can and will if you work the steps. How? Honesty, open-mindedness and willingness. You may discover that you are not as different from others as you might think, that like yourself, we all are looking for support and love, for strength and purpose, our anchor, to reach beyond ourselves to connect with others, for the courage to accept the things we cannot change, the courage to change the things we can, and the wisdom to know the difference.

D.B.'s STORY

I will tell you what it was like, what happened, and what it is like now. I grew up on a farm in South America, with 16 brothers and sisters who were all from the same mother and father. I was the tenth child. I cannot blame my parents for my alcoholism. My parents instilled strong core values such as honesty, respect, hard work, education, and humility. They were outstanding members and leaders of our community. We are Hindus, but my parents were very liberal minded. We hosted Christian Sunday school at our home for people from all different races and religions. My parents did not have any bias toward people. My father and mother taught all of us acceptance. The values they instilled remain with me forever, although I misplaced these when I was drinking.

My parents were well to do, but times got tough after the great depression. Although as children we could not get the things that we always wanted, we always had enough to eat and wear. We grew up on a farm and everyone had to do their share of the work. My father was not always a heavy drinker; actually, in his early years, he discouraged people from drinking. But he became a heavy drinker later in life, although he did not drink continuously. In fact, he could go for years without a drink, but when he finally did, he would drink for several weeks straight. He could be miserable if he was not getting his drink when he wanted more. I know that research has revealed there is a genetic element to the disease of alcoholism, but in spite of this, not everyone in my family went on to drink alcohol or became an alcoholic. I cannot speak about whether anyone else is an alcoholic or not. I can only speak for myself. I have learned that my life works best when I take my own inventory, not yours. It is as simple as that.

I came to Canada when I was 21. I cannot remember when I started to drink but it was an early age. I am not sure when I started to have blackouts.

In Canada, while I was drinking, I was still working hard. I was a very dedicated worker. This came from my core values; however the alcohol got in the way. I just could not help my self; the alcohol just took over. I went to several colleges and earned a couple of certificates, and I had a good head on my shoulders. Unfortunately, I was more interested in the alcohol and fun. I could not say no to drinking and fun with friends. The fact is that I placed drinking and friends in front of my family, school and work.

I had a lot of great jobs, worked with remarkable people and I did a lot of volunteer work and served the community. I even received several awards and recognition. I was not drinking all the time. In the early stages, I was a functional alcoholic. I could drink and no one knew, at least that is what I thought. I worked as a bus driver, professional landscaper, machinist and pool operator. I drove professional sports players to events and met some of the world's greatest cricket players. I had the privilege of being in the company of senior level executives, both in and out of government.

But when I stared to drink more heavily and crossed the line, I could not remember where I was, when I woke up, or how I got there. My memory of some of those times is not so good, but I do remember swearing that I would never do it again. But I did. I kept on repeating myself, even though I said I would not. My father was killed by a drunk driver. I thought I was drinking socially, but I always got drunk.

My marriage lasted six years, and during that time I was drinking heavily. Although I could not function properly, I did not know how to stop. When I had my drink in me I did not care about anything else. During this time I was a bus driver. In spite of it being risky, some days I went to work with a hangover. My drinking eventually caused my marriage to break down. I only had one son, and my wife told me I would not be able to see him until I stopped drinking. So I stopped drinking for several years because I longed to see my son. During this time I felt much better. I tried to reconcile with my wife, but it did not work. The drink was more important than my other responsibilities. I was able to justify everything with the drinking even when I hurt the people who I loved. I moved to Alberta as I thought a new environment will help me to get my life together. While in Alberta I worked as a landscaper for four years. I was drinking on a daily basis and always made excuses for why I was not always punctual or performing my work properly. I was unable to see and believe that alcohol had anything to do with my problems, but I always lied about how much I drank. I was also an excellent cricket player. I played in a cricket league. We drank before, during and after the game. In spite of this I scored several cricket centuries, but in most cases I could not remember these successful cricket innings.

My drinking eventually resulted in me losing my driver's license for two years. As a matter of fact I had filed an application with 'Pardons Canada' to clear my impaired record, but a few days before I was cleared I lost my license again. I eventually came back to Toronto and got another job driving a bus. I was an excellent worker, punctual and dedicated, but I eventually got in a dispute with management over something foolish. While driving one day, I saw a piece of wire on the road that I thought I could use at home. Pulling over, I took it on the bus. The problem was there was a policy prohibiting this and as a result, I lost my job. I then got a job as a facility operator, maintaining swimming pools and getting rooms cleaned for different types of functions. Everything started off extremely well. As usual I worked hard and I received many compliments from the patrons. But the drinking got in the way. One day I had too much to drink and I did not know what I was doing. I really could not remember the incident; however I was told that people complained and called the authorities. When the police came, they charged me with drinking in a public facility and once again, I lost my job and found myself out of work.

I also had a second marriage that failed shortly after I lost my job.

One night, while driving home drunk, I parked my truck on someone else's lawn, two houses away from mine. I was so drunk I did not realize where I was and spent several hours walking up and down the street looking for my home.

The police were called and put me in a paddy wagon before carting me off to jail for the evening. I can tell you that I would rather die than go back to that place. Jail is for animals, not humans.

I did not sleep at all that night.

My brother told me about a treatment center and made arrangements for me to go for treatment. I went there for 21 days. That is where I learned about Alcoholics Anonymous. It is the greatest gift in the world.

The people there taught me what it was like to be like a real human being, not a fake human being, or an animal. When I was drinking, I was unable to tell the difference between truth and fantasy. I was always in denial, and blaming someone else for my troubles. My problem was not when I had the alcohol; it was when I did not have the alcohol. I learned that every person is responsible for their own happiness and unhappiness. I learned that you need to be able to love yourself first before you can love others. I learned that charity begins at home and that the gold mine is usually in your own backyard. It is within each of us. I learned to appreciate things and to be thankful for my blessings.

When I was in denial, I did not know if I was going, coming, or what I was doing. Thanks to Alcoholics Anonymous, today I know what I am doing and I have a purpose: to be a real person. If I do not take a drink today, everything else is a bonus. My Higher Power was always with me, even when I was drinking. I just did not know it. Today, my Higher Power is with me always. I can feel it. Look around, it is all around you.

Alcoholics Anonymous is profound. Everything about it: the loyalty, the truth, the graciousness of people. They always encourage you to keep coming back, and never neglect you. They never refuse you, or discriminate against you. I was an animal when I was drinking, but now I am a human being. I am allergic to dishonesty. I was a scamp, liar, and a thief. I could never be loyal to anyone because I was always disloyal to myself.

Here, in Alcoholics Anonymous, I am able to learn from other people how to be real. Today I can be me. Today I am free. I continue to go to meetings because I am now able to accept that I have a problem, rather than deny it. I get strength and power from the people who are there with me in the meetings. I can choose to go to meetings, or I can choose not to go; I choose to go, however, because every time I do I come away with a different mindset that puts me in the right direction of not picking up a drink. As I say, every time I do not pick up a drink, anything that comes beyond is a bonus.

Today I can be a contributing member of society. The core values my parents taught me are back with me. I went back to school and earned my diploma in addictions studies. Today I am able to speak victory, not defeat. I see the positive, not the negative. When I was drinking, all I could see was the bottom of the bottle; nothing else mattered. I craved the bottle; the bottle did not crave me. Today I am responsible, I am thankful, I mean what I say and say what I mean. And I do not have to say it in a mean way. I do not have to run away from anyone. I can say yes, I did do that, or no, I did not do that.

We live in a great country with a variety of options to give you the help you need and the choice is yours. You have unlimited and endless choices. I cannot cure my disease, but I can overcome it.

Today I have gratitude, which is a gift that cannot be bought. I am now able to admit that I have a mental disease. When I first came into the program I was unable to focus on my reading, but now I can focus and read. Every action has a reaction. You cannot plant corn and pick pears. Ten seconds of pleasure can cause a lifetime of misery but the Lord's Prayer tells me that if I am honest and real, and follow my Higher Power, I cannot go wrong. Like Bob Marley says, you cannot hide from the Father of Creation. I cannot change the past, but today I can overcome me. I can live a life without destruction or obstruction and live a clear life. I keep going to meetings to learn from all of you, my friends and extended family. Today, I am responsible for my actions. My Higher power is always with me. Today is a gift. Today I can accept me, and that is the greatest freedom.

You Can Run, You Can Hide,
You Can Cover, but You Can't Get Away

This chapter corresponds to the first step in The Big Book: "We admitted we were powerless over alcohol . . . that our lives had become unmanageable."

The principle underlying Step One is honesty. You either are, or are not in the grip of a power greater than yourself, and if you are an alcoholic, you are in its grip. As the late, great American boxer Joe Louis said, "You can ride but you cannot hide." No matter where you go, whatever city, town, or country you may live in, there you will be. Your mind follows you wherever you go. You cannot escape your own mind forever, although a lot of us have done that temporarily, consciously or unconsciously through drinking alcohol. Once you crossed the line that separates the alcoholic from the non-alcoholic, you cannot go back. An analogy will help illustrate this statement.

If you dip a cucumber in brine, at some point during the marinating process it becomes a pickle. Once there, the change is irreversible.

The pickle cannot go back and become a cucumber. Alcoholics are like cucumbers that have had too much brine and have become pickles.

Step One is only the beginning of the process, and the first step, like picking up a desire chip to stop drinking, takes honesty to admit defeat.

D.B. drank until he spun so far out of control he found himself chained to others in a paddy waggon and then went on to experience a night in jail. D.B. says he would rather die than go back to jail.

Doc continued to drink until he felt that he was on the edge of an abyss, looking into a bottomless pit, and felt that he was on the verge of losing his soul. D.B. and Doc were both defeated. They could no longer hide or run away.

The Disease of Alcoholism

A disease is an abnormal biological process. You, the "I Am," are a body with biological processes housed in a soul. We cannot see the soul, even though we can sense it. We can, however, see and feel our bodies. All human beings start off as a single cell, consisting of genetic material from both the mother and father. Then, through an incredibly awesome and immensely complex process of ordered wisdom, one cell multiplies to become the approximately 75-100 trillion cells of your body. Each of those cells is destined to become a certain part of your body, and you have approximately 85-100 billion nerve cells with trillions of connections. Life itself is a miracle.

The cells of your body require water, oxygen and food to function properly. Alcohol is a chemical and it affects the cells in your body. Chronic and heavy alcoholism contributes to many illnesses, including heart disease, cancer, and stroke. The cells of your body are trying to keep you alive; however, persistent use of alcohol causes those cells to change the way they operate. At some point . . . which is different for all of us . . . the machinery of the cells is irreversibly changed. The cucumber becomes a pickle.

The nature of the disease of alcoholism is twofold: First, there is a progression whereby the cells of the body desire more and more alcohol. This phenomenon is the craving of the body. Second, the mind becomes preoccupied with satisfying this craving. This is the phenomenon of obsession. There you have it: craving of the body and obsession of the mind.

Cravings and obsessions are progressive, meaning they only move in one direction: they get stronger and more intense. They never get weaker when you drink alcohol. Only you can tell if you are having these experiences. There are many checklists and well-designed questionnaires that you can answer to help determine if you have the disease or not, but the most critical factor noted in The Big Book, and continuously emphasized by D.B. is your willingness to be honest. If you are honest, you will be able to determine if you have the disease. This is true whether you are a man or woman. Your race, creed, and religion do not matter, and neither does your education.

Alcoholism is an equal-opportunity disease, and the potential for honesty is a universal human trait.

You, Me, and We

Doc asked D.B. why The Big Book uses the word "We." D.B. looked at Doc and asked what his first feeling was when he arrived in the Alcoholics Anonymous room. Doc said that people were being real and honest while discussing their emotional pain and the negative impact of alcohol on their lives. D.B. asked, "What else?" Doc didn't know, so D.B. said: "You are no longer alone and have to suffer in isolation. A problem half shared is a problem half-solved."

Upon hearing this, Doc felt he could breathe a little easier.

D.B. explained that the "We" in the first step meant that we no longer had to run. We no longer had to cover and hide. We could admit something about ourselves that we did not want to admit. He said others in the room who were in recovery were not only willing to listen, but that in the process of listening, it was actually helping the listener as much as the speaker.

D.B. said alcoholics tend to be isolationists and lone rangers, constructing a prison around us while not realizing we are the prisoners. By coming together and sharing our stories, we come out of the prison of isolation. We are no longer alone.

"Powerlessness" and "Unmanageability"

Before Doc was ready to open up, he pressed on and asked for a definition of powerlessness, insisting it did not apply to him since he had free will.

D.B. asked Doc to hold his breath.

"For how long?" Doc asked.

"For as long as you can."

Doc went on to tell D.B. that as a child, he tried this several times in the swimming pool, at one point thinking that maybe he could be like a fish and breathe under water. Although he tried his best to imagine he was a fish with gills instead of lungs, it obviously did not work. At some point, the pressure just became too much and Doc had to get some air.

D.B. said, "Well, there you go."

Doc looked puzzled. D.B. went on to explain that if he had the power to breathe under water, he would have been able to do it, but as much as he wanted it, he did not have that power. Doc understood the biology involved, that the cells of the brain were accumulating carbon dioxide and that when too much carbon dioxide accumulated, the cells in his brain sent out an alarm signal to the lungs demanding oxygen; and no matter how much Doc fantasized or imagined that he was a fish, he was not going to get away from the fact that he was a human with lungs, not gills. That's why D.B. said "You cannot get away. You are what you are; accept that."

"Give me another example," Doc demanded.

D.B. thought for a moment and then asked Doc how long he could go without sleep, or without water and food.

"How long can you drive your car before you have to fill up with gas?" he asked. "The car is powerless without gas, and you are powerless to go without sleep, water, or food for an extended period of time. At some point, your body will simply not be able to do it; at that point, you are powerless."

D.B. smiled, raised his eyebrows with a self-assured manner, and then asked Doc to tell him where he had been powerless over alcohol.

Doc felt grateful he could be honest and that his memory provided him instances of where and when he was powerless.

He remembered a situation of "where" before going to watch his younger son play soccer. He said to himself that he would not drink alcohol, and he really meant it. However, by the time the game ended, Doc had several drinks and afterwards drove home with his children in the car. By the grace of God, there were no accidents.

Doc shivered in fright and bewilderment as he thought about the craziness, the foolishness, and the insanity of his actions on that day.

In spite of this, Doc continued to insist that he was not powerless. D.B. said, "Tell me more."

Doc remembered how he used to hide bottles of alcohol in the house, and the feeling of being sneaky while doing this.

"Why were you sneaky?" he asked. "And why did you have to hide the bottles?"

Doc really didn't know. Although he felt shame, it was coupled with a strong desire to defend and justify his actions, which caused him to remain silent, as if a deeper voice was telling him to wait.

D.B. said, "Tell me more."

Doc said he noticed he began looking forward to drinking on Friday nights and promising himself he would not drink as much on the weekends. When he looked honestly at his memories, however, . . . and D.B. emphasized that he was allergic to dishonesty . . . Doc realized that his drinking progressed, just as The Big Book said it would; he eventually found himself drinking on Saturdays, Sundays, and then Mondays. Then a few late lunches, all of which were accompanied by a sense of unease when he did not have alcohol, of being restless, irritable and discontented when he did not have his stash. When Doc was brutally honest, he was able to see that his mental life was being progressively consumed by thoughts of getting alcohol when he did not have it.

D.B. asked, "Are you powerless?"

Doc still didn't like the word. He was too proud to admit it, and unwilling to surrender, yet he knew in the deepest part of himself that he always wanted more and more alcohol. It had not always been that way, but at some point, Doc crossed an invisible line where he became an alcoholic.

Doc sensed the grace of a Higher Power when his intuition told him that his drinking would only progress and that his life would only be filled with greater problems if he continued. Doc knew he was in a pickle, that he was a pickle.

D.B. said, "Give me one more example."

Doc remembered one time where he went out to dinner with his family. After paying the bill and leaving the restaurant, when they got in the car he lied and told his wife that he forgot to give the waiter a tip. When he went back inside, he angrily demanded that the waiter rush and give him another two beers, which Doc then proceeded to gulp down quickly.

D.B. looked at Doc and said, "You can run, you can cover, you can hide, but you cannot get away."

At that moment Doc knew that he was powerless over alcohol, and that his life was unmanageable. Doc was living a double life, characterized by deceit and lies. He may have looked just fine on the outside, but he felt as if the foundation of his life was crumbling underneath him.

"That is the unmanageability," D.B. said. "You no longer have the power on the inside to feel peace and serenity."

Just as Doc was feeling more down and out, knowing he was defeated, D.B. smiled a big knowing and assuring smile.

"Good," he said. "You have the gift of desperation. The best is yet to come. We still have 11 more steps."

What is Denial?

One of the gifts of sobriety is the ability to think rationally, logically, systematically, and perhaps most importantly, honestly. Given the good times that people have with alcohol—at least in the early stages—there is a tendency for the mind to only look at the good times while ignoring the bad experiences. For example, when D.B. asked Doc to honestly tell him about his drinking experiences, Doc could have focused on the laughter and the song, the feelings of courage and power, and the fine physical feeling of a buzz, or a high: what The Big Book calls an elusive feeling. Doc could also have pointed out and emphasized that everyone gets into a scrap here and there, or that he is no different than other people. He could have gone on to say that no one is without sin and temptation, thus deflecting attention away from himself and the cause-and-effect relationship between alcohol and his own problems. He could have attempted to point out that he is not like that person on skid row with a raincoat and paper bag. Even if D.B. told Doc that he could metaphorically get off the elevator before it hit the ground floor, Doc would not have been able to see what the ground floor looked like.

Denial is not being able to fast-forward the mind and see the logical and future outcome resulting from today's negative actions.

Denial, as it relates to the disease of alcoholism, is not seeing the potential danger that is about to unfold, even if others tell you about it. How can this be? In denial, one continues drinking because of the compulsion of the craving or the obsession of the mind.

Denial is also what happens when a person knows that there is a danger lurking in the distance and despite realizing it is best to avoid the danger, still proceeds forward.

By way of illustration, Doc remembers driving his son to a baseball game while saying to himself that he will not drink alcohol while driving. However, once at the baseball game, Doc secretly goes to a Johnny-on-the-spot to drink alcohol. Denial is not even considering that this is hardly a place to be doing anything but what is meant to be done. At the end of the game, even though Doc had too much to drink and is legally over the limit, he manages to convince himself that he still has his full mental faculties, and is in control so there is nothing to worry about. He then drives home with his son in the car, never giving any serious thought about the potentially devastating consequences of driving under the influence.

Denial is the opposite of logical, thoughtful, disciplined thinking about oneself, others, and the impact of one's behavior on others and on one's life. It is a narrowing of vision to think only of self, and what one can do, rather than what one should do. Denial is like living under a concrete roof and not being able to see the sunshine of reason. Denial also occurs when we cannot see our own responsibility for our problems.

With respect to the scenario noted above, what about the voice within, the "I Am" telling Doc that this is a bad decision? Well, either that voice has become silenced by the alcohol and does not even come into conscious awareness or, alternatively, Doc rationalizes and defends his actions from a narrow, self-centered perspective, driven by a need to continue to have the right to drink.

The key here is that when an alcoholic is in denial, the interpretation given to any situation will always be one that justifies the continued use of alcohol. The alcohol has become the master. The person in denial thinks he is the master when, in reality, he is a slave.

There is an expression in the rooms of Alcoholics Anonymous: 'play the tape to the end.'

If you are in denial, you either cannot or will not play the tape forward. However, once you recognize you are powerless over alcohol and that your life has become unmanageable, you are able to begin the process of halting a negative, downward spiral. You become ready to surrender your past and to be open to a future that you cannot yet imagine, one that is filled with something better than you could have imagined.

What Do You Remember?

The mind can be used as a carefully calibrated instrument which can move in any direction the individual chooses. You can defend any position with which you start out, and rationalize any decision you have made. Denial is when you recall only the good experiences in your drinking, and forget the negative consequences or outcomes.

Why do you think people do this? Thinking otherwise might result in the person having to reduce or stop his or her drinking. Although a person may consciously say he or she wants to do this, deep down, they are not sincere.

Alcohol can be an escape from life but if you are in denial you do not see this. You do not remember that alcohol allowed you to escape from feelings of restlessness, irritability, or discontentment.

If you stop drinking alcohol for any period of time, take note of the feelings you experience. Are you happy, joyous, and free? Are you able to cope with the stressors in your life? Are you able to deal with the persistent, intrusive, and unwelcome thoughts that race into your mind?

Remember, if you have not had a drink of alcohol for some period of time—if you have truly crossed an invisible line—the cells of the body will have changed irreversibly. Once you put the drink back into your body, you will kick-start the dual process of physical craving and mental obsession all over again. In order to see this, you need only look carefully and honestly at your experiences, or go to a meeting and listen to others who have fallen back into drinking and their experiences. Are you ready to look honestly at yourself?

Hitting a Bottom

It is the very nature of the disease of alcoholism that, after the cells have changed, the person hungers, yearns, and often angrily insists that there is nothing wrong. When in denial, you do not see the cause-and-effect relationship of alcohol and the problems it brings.

In these circumstances, the mind defends, rationalizes, and justifies the continued use of alcohol. Until you are sick and tired of being sick and tired, you may not realize that you have truly crossed the line from being a cucumber to a pickle.

Neither D.B. nor Doc would have listened to others until they hit their bottom. That is why no one can tell you that you are powerless or whether your life is unmanageable. You have to discover it for yourself. We ask you to consider, however, that when you do your examination, remember that you do not have to go to the bottom floor of the elevator before you get off.

Unfortunately, we sometimes have to learn things the hard way.

Normal drinkers stop when they see their drinking is bringing about bad outcomes. Alcoholics, however, continue to drink even when there is an increased conflict with others, job loss, legal problems, or an overwhelming sense of impending doom. Alcoholics do not see the cause-and-effect relationship between their alcohol use and their negative experiences. Alcoholics do not change until they have hit their bottom. Step One is about recognizing your bottom, how you are powerless over alcohol, and how your life has become unmanageable.

Questions to Consider

We encourage you to write your answers to these questions and then to discuss them with someone you trust. This is the best way to avoid denial.

1. How often do you drink?
2. What do you drink for? What do you hope to get from your drinking?
3. What do you like about yourself when you drink?
4. What do you not like about yourself when you drink?
5. Do you feel a physical craving once you start or stop?
6. How much do you think about alcohol when you are not drinking? (Hint: normal drinkers do not think about alcohol when they are not drinking alcohol.)

7. Do you have to be secretive about your drinking? Sneaky?

8. Have you hit a bottom with alcohol? What is your bottom?

9. Regarding unmanageability, do you feel well-rested and calm, or do you feel a sense of anxiety or panic? Provide specific examples in your personal and work lives.

Summary

Step One corresponds to honesty—honesty about your powerlessness over alcohol and about where your life has become unmanageable.

We emphasize that it does not matter how many days, months, or years you have been sober. As The Big Book says, our sobriety is contingent on our spiritual condition, one day at a time. It is not enough to understand this; practicing it is better, as D.B. would say.

To practice the step is to honestly examine where and when you have hit bottom, and whether you are willing to surrender and admit defeat. When you take Step One, you are moving from denial to reality, from having a fake self to discovering your true self.

As D.B. says, "The choice is yours."

You Can't Change Your Disease but You Can Overcome it

This chapter corresponds to the second step in The Big Book: "Came to believe that a Power greater than ourselves could restore us to sanity."

The principle underlying Step Two is hope. As discussed in Chapter 1, the disease of alcoholism is progressive. It always gets worse, never better. Once you have crossed the invisible line of drinking alcoholically, which is a form of insanity, your cells have changed irreversibly. Just as you cannot change the law of gravity, or plant corn and pick pears, you cannot change the nature of your disease. However, you can connect and access a power that gives you the strength and courage to move beyond the disease, and takes you to a different understanding and experience of yourself to a higher, spiritual dimension. You do not change your disease. You tap into a power that transforms you, not the disease. You move beyond your disease; you overcome it.

Came to Believe

When you come to believe something which you previously did not know or had never been exposed to it, you are opening your mind to new ideas and new ways of thinking. It is a process of coming to know something, and as this idea relates to Step Two, that something is very special.

The process of "coming to believe" requires active listening.

There is a difference between passive and active listening. Passive listening is hearing the words, while active listening involves hearing the words and feelings, and trying to understand more deeply what is being said.

Have you ever felt the difference when someone seemed to be pretending to listen to you as opposed to when they were really listening to you and trying to enter into your frame of reference—your world? The feeling of being "listened to" is reassuring and comforting.

When D.B. and Doc became sober, they initially discovered they did not have the patience to listen to others. The chatter of thoughts racing in their minds prevented them from listening to a deeper message that was coming from somewhere else—their souls.

D.B. and Doc have discovered that when they did Step One and became honest with themselves, they were just beginning to listen to themselves differently: without the clouded haze of alcohol distortion. Although it was just a beginning, they began to hear the voice of their own conscience, the "I Am,"—their true selves.

The Big Book says that more and more will be revealed to us once we are on a spiritual path of recovery. How much more will be revealed to you depends on your willingness to listen and to receive the message, the insight, and the intuition that is being sent. The message, the intuition, the insight and the feeling is being sent to you and through you by a Power greater than yourself. You get to discover and define what that Power is for you.

A Power Greater Than Yourself

The word "power" means "a force, an energy." Some examples of power include gravity, electricity, and solar energy. The power of the sun provides the energy of light that allows plants to make the sugar and oxygen. You breathe the oxygen necessary for survival and breathe out carbon dioxide. The plants use that carbon dioxide, along with energy—power—from sunlight to make food necessary for growth and oxygen. It is a cycle, and you are part of the cycle. You are part of, and connected to, that power.

The earth as we know it would not survive without the sun.

You did not make the sun or any of the other planets. While there may be differences of opinion about how the sun first came into existence, what you know for sure is that neither you nor any of your friends were the power that caused it.

Here is one more example of a power greater than yourself: every one of your approximately 75-100 trillion cells in your body, with the exception of the sex and blood cells, is making approximately 2,000 proteins every second. A protein is a combination of 300 to more than 1,000 amino acids. Every second of every minute of every day, your body is manufacturing 150 thousand, thousand, thousand, thousand, thousand thousand amino acids into carefully-designed proteins, every second; every minute of every day, right now. That is a power greater than yourself even though you are a part of, and connected to, that power.

The two examples above relate to a physical power, but what about a spiritual power? When we talk of a spiritual power, we are talking about principles, and the power that enables you to connect to these principles. Over the years, a list of 12 principles, each corresponding to one of the Twelve Steps, has been printed in AA newsletters and pocket cards.

Step One	Honesty
Step Two	Hope
Step Three	Faith
Step Four	Courage
Step Five	Integrity
Step Six	Willingness
Step Seven	Humility
Step Eight	Brotherly and Sisterly Love
Step Nine	Justice
Step Ten	Perseverance
Step Eleven	Spiritual Awareness
Step Twelve	Service

It is pretty amazing to think that you are made up of physical matter but the principles noted above are not physical; they are spiritual. The brain gives rise to the mind. The brain is physical; the mind is spiritual. However, you have to tap into that rich treasure, the treasure of your soul.

Doc asked D.B. why he couldn't tap into this treasure and drink alcohol at the same time. He said that it does not work that way because alcohol clouds the mind and interferes with the ability to make the connection with a Power greater than yourself. Doc wanted to know why. D.B. answered that he did not know; that's just the way it works, he said.

Compare it to gravity.

"Objects fall down, not up," he says. "You cannot plant corn and pick a pear. Water freezes at 0° C, no other number, at least here on earth."

"Why?" Doc asked. "Why, why, why?"

"It's great that you are asking questions, Doc," he said. "Study science; it is the `how' of the physical universe, but the 'why' is something that you are going to have to find out yourself because it is personal and relates to your own journey of discovery—your own purpose."

"When you begin working Step Two, and finding a Power greater than yourself," D.B. said, "you will begin to discover the why, the "I Am," that is the real you, not the fake you."

D.B. then went on to explain that you can choose a Higher Power of your own understanding, as long as it is not you. D.B. said that for some people the word "God" stands as an acronym for "good orderly direction."

Doc said he did not understand how someone could know when he or she is making connection with this Power. "It is simple,"

D.B. said, and asked Doc to come to a meeting of Alcoholics Anonymous with him. At the meeting, people went around the room and everyone had a chance to speak about Step Two and what it meant to them. Each person listened when the other spoke. Doc found his attention wandering at times; other times, someone would say something that triggered him to have a thought and a feeling different from the ones he was feeling before he went to the meeting.

Some people seemed to be going through a difficult time, while others were having more positive experiences. Doc could not quite explain why but he noted that he felt better after the meeting. D.B. said that Doc could think of the sharing of other members and the honesty in the rooms of Alcoholics Anonymous, as a Power greater than himself because that Power made Doc feel better.

Doc began to think about being drunk one night and how the thought came to him that he needed to be around honest people.

This thought came to Doc's mind unannounced, and it was so overpowering that he travelled more than 50 kilometres to a meeting of Alcoholics Anonymous. D.B. said that perhaps the thought that Doc had was a sort of Power giving guidance. Doc then had an image of his late parents, of blessed memory, and he realized that the love he associated with that memory was a sort of anchor, a Power with which he could connect.

D.B. reminded Doc that this Power would and could strengthen a person in a good way, and provide support to stay sober, one day at a time. D.B. went on to say that while this Power could and would help Doc do the next right thing, ultimately it was Doc's choice whether he wanted to do the next right thing or not. D.B. told Doc to keep coming back, meaning keep coming to the rooms to hear the message of hope, which gets expressed in so many different ways by so many different people.

"Keep an open mind," D.B. said, "and keep listening and sharing. If you keep searching for this Power, you will find it, and it will find you. Just keep an open mind. The Higher Power of your understanding, if you search for it, will help you keep sober. Be kind to yourself, Doc."

Doc asked why he wrote "Power" with a capital "P" rather than a small "p." He said the reason is because it is greater than himself.

D.B. laughed as he then said, "and besides, the Higher Power of your understanding will restore you to sanity."

What is Sanity?

Sanity is soundness of mind and judgment. Sanity is being able to use your powers of reasoning and thinking in a rational manner, with a willingness to look at situations from different perspectives apart from your own. It is natural that no two people will necessarily see or interpret a situation the same way. Sane thinking and behavior reflects a willingness to recognize the many different feelings and emotions that may be influencing your decision. It is a willingness and ability to feel your feelings without having to act impulsively. It is thinking about the potential consequences of your behaviour on yourself and others.

Doc had a really difficult time accepting that he needed to be restored to sanity. After all, he told D.B., he still had his family and his job. Doc said that maybe he was lucky. D.B. said, "No, you are not lucky; you are fortunate. The disease of alcoholism is progressive.

You should consider using the word 'yet,' because if you continued to drink, you very well could have lost everything, just as some people tragically have done. If you are not on a path to recovery, you are on a path to jail, institutions, and death."

"But I am not insane," Doc insisted. "Insanity is when people hear voices and act crazy."

"Well," D.B. said, "maybe you didn't hear voices, but let's look at your experience of drinking and decide if it is crazy or normal.

Remember when you told me that before you went to a dinner with your wife and two children you secretly had several drinks? And then during dinner you went on to drink to such an extent that the waitress at one point told you she was not going to give you any more drinks, causing you to get angry. Did you stop and think on how your anger affected the waitress? Your wife? Your children?

And what about after you paid the bill and left the restaurant with your family? When you got in the car, you lied and told your wife that you forgot to give the waiter a tip. You were angry, went back to the restaurant, and rudely demanded that the waiter rush and give you another two beers, which you proceeded to gulp down quickly.

"When you got back to the car, you lied again."

"Do you think that is normal and sane, or crazy and insane?" D.B. asked.

Doc certainly did not like the word insane but he begrudgingly accepted the fact that normal people would not do this. D.B. told him to substitute the word "crazy" for "insanity" if he wished.

D.B. said he felt that his own drinking was insane because when he was not able to get the alcohol, he would lay down and act like an animal. He said he would lie, cheat, steal, or do whatever he needed to do to get the alcohol. He could not think straight or logically, or care about the effect of his behavior on others. He could not identify any emotion other than anger and he could not stop thinking about anything else besides the alcohol when he did not have it.

"I think that is pretty much insane," he said.

Doc thought again about how he found the rooms of Alcoholics Anonymous for the first time, of how he felt overwhelmed and nervous thinking that his life was crumbling apart, even though on the outside everything may have looked fine. Doc thought about how he needed to be around honest people and that he did not know why or how that thought came to him, but it caused him to drive 50 kilometers away from his home to a meeting. He went on to think about how he felt he could breathe a little easier once he got to the meeting, and how his thoughts stopped racing so quickly. Doc thought about how people came up to him after the meeting with smiles and handshakes while expressing a positive and kindly glow, telling him they were glad he was there and that he did not have to be concerned about what he did tomorrow, that he just did not have to drink for that day. He thought about how in that moment he felt a little bit more at peace, that there was some force, something in those rooms that was safe and that he wanted what others had. Looking back at that memory, Doc felt deeply—not just on the surface—that some Power, a Higher Power of his own understanding, (however limited that understanding), was greater than himself, and could restore him to sanity.

Questions to Consider

1. What do you believe in?
2. How do you believe that your drinking alcohol has affected your thinking, feeling, and behaving?
3. What is your understanding of the word power?
4. What is your understanding of the phrase, "Power greater than ourselves?"
5. What is your understanding of the words, "sanity" and "insanity?"
6. Did you ever drink in an insane manner?
7. What is your understanding of the phrase, "could restore us to sanity?"
8. What is the way that you connect to a Power greater than yourself? How does this help you to remain physically and emotionally sober?

Summary

Recovery from the grip of alcoholism requires you to have the power to think, feel, and act differently. If you knew how to do this on your own, through your own power, you would have already done it. Some people think they can do it on their own and if they can that is wonderful. If you have done Step One, however, and discovered that you cannot, then Step Two is about finding a Higher Power of your understanding that can assist you. You do not have to figure this out all by yourself. That is why the word "us" is used in Step Two instead of "you."

One great way to work Step Two is to go to meetings. While there, you share what is in your mind and heart and you listen to others. You begin to identify with others and see that you are no longer alone, that you belong. Others will also benefit from your sharing in ways you may not even know.

Your life will get better when you put the plug in the chug. You will think more clearly and feel more deeply. This does not mean circumstances will always work out the way you want. The promise of the program is that as long as you stay close to it and do one thing every day related to the steps, you may not get what you want, but you will get what you need. Doc learned this from Simon, a fellow traveller in the program.

While you're in the program, there are people who will celebrate with you in your successes and provide support and comfort when you hurt. Some moments may feel unmanageable but as time goes on the periods will not be as long or as severe, and you will have the tools to deal with it.

You may not be able to change your disease of alcoholism, but you will be able to overcome it with the help of others, the fellowship, and a Higher Power of your own understanding. There is hope.

When you do Step Two, you will not only be removed from the alcoholic craving of the body and the obsession of the mind, you will no longer live with a sense of impending calamity. You will be restored to sanity.

As D.B. says, "The choice is yours."

There is One Original; the Rest is Carbon Copy

This chapter corresponds to the third step in The Big Book: "Made a decision to turn our will and our lives over to the care of God *as we understood Him.*"

The principle behind Step Three is faith. Faith is having belief but not necessarily having proof. After nearly one year in the program, while coming out of a meeting, someone sarcastically asked D.B., "Who do you think you are, Mr. AA?!"

It was in that particular moment that D.B. had an awakening, a moment of clarity. He realized that although he could talk the talk, he was not walking the walk, and that he couldn't ever really do this until he surrendered his will to that of his Higher Power.

D.B. realized that it was his Higher Power's will that would be done in this earth and heaven, not his. Though neither D.B. or Doc are Christians, D.B. referenced the words of the Christian prayer, commonly referred to as the Lord's Prayer.

"Our Father, who art in heaven, hallowed be thy name. Thy kingdom come, thy will be done, in earth as it is in heaven. Give us this day our daily bread, and forgive us our trespasses, as we forgive those who trespass against us. And lead us not into temptation, but deliver us from evil: For thine is the kingdom, the power, and the glory, forever and ever. Amen."

D.B. reminded Doc that if these words do not speak to someone in the program, that is fine. Each person could choose whatever prayer works for him or her.

D.B. went on to note The Big Book referenced Bill W. as having a spiritual awakening, where for a brief moment, "I had needed and wanted God. There had been a humble willingness to have Him with me – and He came." (page 12 of The Big Book of Alcoholics Anonymous).

Bill W. then noted that the sense of "His presence had been blotted out by worldly clamours, mostly those within myself (pages 12-13)."

D.B. says he doesn't exactly know what happened, but it was like a switch went on inside him. He realized that he will always have his temptations, struggles and internal conflicts. He could stop the fight and surrender. He could turn his will over to his Higher Power for guidance, for comfort and support to do the next right thing. Knowing that while everything on the outside may not be okay, everything would be fine as long as he tried to stay connected to his Higher Power. D.B. believed the promises of the program—a new freedom and happiness—would come true; however, he realized he had to work for them, and they weren't going to happen in D.B.'s timeframe. They would happen in his Higher Power's timeframe.

Each person who works the steps experiences their spiritual awakening in their own way, in their own place, and in their own time.

Remember that Step Three refers to "God as we understood Him."

This leaves the door wide open for your own spiritual awakening experience. For some, the spiritual awakening happens quickly and suddenly. For others, it occurs gradually, but The Big Book promises it will always happen when a person is working all the steps. Faith is allowing yourself to know that it will happen for you too, if you really want it to and if you work the steps.

When D.B. refers to an original and a carbon copy, he is saying that your will and desires have given you pleasures and satisfactions, as well as troubles and grief. It is but a carbon copy of some false self, and not your true self. Your true self is your original self, before it went off rioting with self-will. The way to get back to your true, original self is to connect with your Higher Power, and to turn your will over to your Higher Power. Faith is making a decision to do this, based on some sense in you that others have been able to reap the fruits of this process—a sense of peace and serenity, a sense of being whole and complete, of being right inside one's own skin, and a sense of being cared for, loved, and protected by a Higher Power.

Made a Decision

When you took Step Two, you had hope that a Power greater than yourself could help you think clearly and with sanity. Now, on Step Three, you are making a decision to allow this Higher Power to help you. A decision is not just wanting something, although that is a good start. A decision is exercising your will.

Doc experienced a moment of grace one night when he was drinking. He'd had too much to drink and his life was spinning out of control. He realized he could not find peace anywhere and was experiencing a sense of impending doom. He had never felt that way before. Then the thought came to him to be around honest people.

Doc did not know where and why that thought came to him, but today he thinks it must have come from his Higher Power. That is why he calls what happened that evening, "grace." This is because Doc did not plan or decide to have this thought, nor did he decide at that point to stop drinking. The moment of grace was being given by a thought from some force greater than himself, some Higher Power that was reaching out to him. For Doc it came in the form of a sudden thought that he would not have come up with on his own.

It was from some Higher Power. Now Doc had to decide what he was going to do with that thought.

You do not choose the first thought that comes to your mind but you do have a choice about what you are going to do with it. Many thoughts come to you in a day, sometimes quietly and sometimes very urgently, all demanding your attention. You have free will. Do you let thoughts run in all directions, or do you meditate and pray for some guidance and peace? Do you call someone else to talk about what is bothering you, or do you keep your secrets to yourself? Do you focus on thoughts of blaming others, or do you think about ways to take responsibility?

D.B. said to Doc: "We are making decisions all the time. When you make a decision you are exercising your will. And remember, we do this one day at a time, one moment at a time. You are human, so you will make some good decisions and some bad decisions. Be kind to yourself, Doc. And try to be kind to others. When you turn your will over to your Higher Power, you will make more good decisions than bad ones. When you turn your will over to your Higher Power, you are making a decision to live a more useful, contented life."

Turning Your Will Over to the Care of Your Higher Power

Doc asked D.B. what it means to turn one's will over to something else. D.B. told him a good first step is to not act impulsively on your first thought. If you have the thought to steal, or to do harm to someone else, turning your will over to your Higher Power means not acting on thoughts that could be harmful to yourself or others.

Doc told D.B. that he could not get the thoughts out of his mind regarding the wrongs he felt he had done in his past and the regrets and worries that he had. D.B. advised him that while he would examine his life more thoroughly when he got to Step Four, for now, Doc would have to have faith that he could ask this Higher Power for help.

"Say the serenity prayer," D.B. said. "Say it over and over again."

"What is the serenity prayer?" Doc asked.

D.B. explained that it was written by the late Reinhold Niebuhr (1892-1971) and over the years it has saved a lot of peoples' lives.

D.B. went on to say it has taken him 10 years just to get a glimpse of the immense power of this prayer.

The serenity prayer: "God, grant me the serenity to accept the things I cannot change, courage to change the things I can, and the wisdom to know the difference."

"Keep saying the serenity prayer, Doc, over and over again," D.B. repeated. "Your Higher Power will answer you, but it may not be in the time frame that you want. Remember, when you made a decision to turn your will over to the care of your Higher Power, you have to trust that this Higher Power is going to help you but you cannot run the show anymore. You have to be humble and wait patiently for the answers. They may come quickly or they may come slowly but they will come. You will know when it is the right answer: when you feel right with yourself."

"How will I know when I feel right with myself?"

"You will know, because your Higher Power gave you intellect, a conscience, and an intuition. Sure, it is probably a good idea that you talk things over with your sponsor before you make big, important decisions. But over time, as you make better and better contact with a Higher Power of your understanding, as The Big Book says, you will intuitively be able to make decisions that used to baffle you. What I like to do is say the serenity prayer. That always helps me to open the connection with my Higher Power. Let's say the serenity prayer together right now: 'God, grant me the serenity to accept the things I cannot change, the courage to change the things I can, and the wisdom to know the difference.'"

"What did you feel when you said the serenity prayer?" D.B. asked.

"Nothing," Doc said.

"Well, keep on saying it over and over again, and go to meetings.

You will feel better."

For the rest of the day, Doc said the serenity prayer over and over. It didn't take away his worries and fears, but at least Doc didn't feel that he had to rush and take a drink. Doc was feeling his feelings, and the thought occurred to him that maybe as a result of feeling what he was feeling, and not having to run away from these feelings or take a drink of alcohol, that perhaps someday he would be able to share his experience with others, and then others might be able to identify with him and not feel so alone. Maybe, Doc thought, this idea itself was coming from his Higher Power, and was evidence that he had made a decision to turn his will over to this Higher Power.

Doc remembered that Simon smiled and told Doc that he did not have to worry about yesterday or tomorrow, just what was in front of him today. Simon said it with peace in his heart, and the conviction that all Doc needed to do was decide to turn over his will, and to try to focus his attention on helping others.

"You cannot control the outcome," he said, "and it will always turn out all right in the long run, even if there are short-term obstacles and you aren't getting what you want."

Like D.B., Simon had faith and told Doc that when he makes a decision to turn his will and life over to his Higher Power, he will realize that he has to do this every day, and sometimes many times during the day.

Simon said that the first thing he does in the morning is ask for help from his Higher Power, asking it to remove his negative and selfish thoughts and to help him find peace and serenity. The last thing he does before going to sleep is to thank his Higher Power for helping him to stay sober.

Simon smiled and chuckled: "I always get what I need from my Higher Power. I don't always get what I want. When all else fails, go to a meeting, greet others, and find a way where you can be of service to others. Get involved in the group. Take on a role, like making coffee or cleaning up. Become the secretary or treasurer of the group. Volunteer to chair or be a speaker. These things are turning your will and care over to your Higher Power."

Doc turned to his sponsor, Les, who told him that he turns his will over by trying to do the next right thing.

"Just do the next right thing," he said. "Don't worry about yesterday or tomorrow, just do the next right thing now. That is turning your will over."

"Be kind to yourself, Doc," D.B. said. "If you cannot be kind to yourself, you cannot be kind to others. Sometimes you can try to do too many things in one day. Rome wasn't built in a day, you know."

Doc and D.B. then talked about the prose, "Yesterday, Today, and Tomorrow." The author is unknown. This prose is read at the meetings.

> *"There are two days in every week about which we should not worry,*
> *Two days which should be kept free from fear and apprehension.*
> *One of these days is Yesterday, with its mistakes and cares,*
> *Its faults and blunders, its aches and pains.*
> *Yesterday has passed forever beyond our control.*
> *All the money in the world cannot bring back Yesterday.*
> *We cannot undo a single act we performed;*
> *We cannot erase a single word we said. Yesterday is gone.*
> *The other day we should not worry about is Tomorrow,*
> *With its possible adversities, its burdens, its large promise and poor performance.*
> *Tomorrow is also beyond our immediate control.*

*Tomorrow's sun will rise, either in splendor or behind a
    mask of clouds, but it will rise.*
*Until it does, we have no stake in Tomorrow, for it is as
    yet unborn.*
This leaves only one day, Today.
Any person can fight the battles of just one day.
*It is only when you and I add the burdens of those two
    awful eternities—*
Yesterday and Tomorrow—that we break down.
It is not the experience of Today that drives a person mad.
It is remorse or bitterness for something which happened

Yesterday
And the dread of what Tomorrow may bring.
Let us therefore live but one day at a time."

The atmosphere in the room became very quiet while the prose was being read. D.B. then said to Doc, "Just because you turned your will over yesterday, doesn't mean you don't have to do it today. You turn your will over every day, sometimes many times during the d   ay, because if your will is like mine it is very self-centered, and I want what I want, when I want it. And remember that Step Three says 'care of God *as we understood Him.'* Your Higher Power will take care of you as long as you surrender to this Higher Power because there is a plan for you better than the one you can create for yourself by your own will. Surrender your power to your Higher Power. It's as simple as that."

Questions to Consider

1. What does making a decision mean to you?

2. What decisions did you make today?
3. What does it mean to you to turn your will and life "over to the care of God *as we understood Him?*"
4. Have you ever tried to turn your will and life over to the care of a Higher Power, even for just a moment? What were the results?
5. Have you asked how others turn their will and their lives over to the care of a Higher Power? What results did they get?

Summary

You make decisions all the time. When you were drinking alcohol, many of the decisions you made were likely shaped and influenced by the physical cravings of needing more alcohol or by the obsessions in your mind. When you did not have the alcohol you may have been preoccupied with thoughts about getting it and when you were drinking, your decisions and range of vision were made narrower because of the alcoholic haze. Making a decision to be sober is a decision to think clearly about your life, your purpose and what you want in life. It is a decision to face your life rather than run from it. It is a decision to say "yes" and "no" with clarity and conviction and peace of mind. It is a decision to reclaim you, the real you, the "I Am" that is the original you, and not a carbon copy of something fake. When you make a decision to turn your will over to your Higher Power, you are asking for help to be relieved of the alcoholic nightmare, and the pain of being alone and isolated, of having to constantly run away from something negative. By saying "yes" to your Higher Power, you are saying "yes" to your original self.

You are saying "yes" to life and to your courage to carry on. You are saying "yes" to love and gratitude. You are saying "yes" to thinking about others as well as yourself. You are surrendering and declaring that you are no longer the director. You are making a decision to have faith to allow your Higher Power to do for you what you cannot do for yourself and discovering in the process that you have the courage and strength to be original, to be the person you always wanted to be. You are making a decision to have faith that you can and will be happy, joyous, and free.

As D.B. says, "The choice is yours."

To Win the Race You've Got To to Win You First

This chapter corresponds to the fourth step in The Big Book: "Made a searching and fearless moral inventory of ourselves."

The principle behind Step Four is courage. All people have fear. It takes courage to face your fears—your fear of losing what you have, your fear of not getting what you want, and your fear of getting something that you don't want. When we work Step Four, we see the connection between fears and resentments along with the downward spiralling of our emotions and lives when we are ruled by these emotions.

When you were drinking alcohol, you probably did not face your fears and resentments or see your part in what caused or maintained them. You got your courage from the bottle but it was false courage and not real courage; it never lasted. That is why the fears and resentments kept returning and you were never able to attain real peace.

When you were drinking alcohol, you may not have had the honesty to recognize that you had fears or resentments, perhaps blocking them out, or at least you tried. As we discussed in the first step, you can run but you cannot hide. Your past will eventually catch up with you just as it does for everyone. When it does, the negative emotions of fear and resentment become your ruler and master, just like alcohol was.

Your mind is like a garden. As D.B. has said, 'you cannot plant corn and pick pears. You cannot think negative thoughts and expect to produce positive results.' To extend the analogy of a garden, as a result of our thoughts and actions some fine plants have grown, but we have also grown useless weeds and poisonous plants. These are our fears and resentments. D.B. told Doc that if he wanted to grow a great garden he would have to get rid of the weeds of fear and the poison of resentment.

"To win the race," D.B. said, "you have got to win you first."

Doc told D.B. that life was not a race and besides, the idea of a race brought up images of being hurried and rushed.

"It is not a rush," he said, "but if you have crossed a line with alcohol, you are in danger. The weeds are racing against you and good plants are dying. Unless you decide to change, unless you have the courage to change, the garden of your mind and soul will be destroyed. To win you first means for you to have the courage to begin to make yourself a better garden. Either the weeds will win the race or you will."

Being Searching and Fearless

Step Four is about having a close look at ourselves, about the things we did and did not do in our lives that have caused pain and hurt to others and ourselves. It is specifically about what we have done right in our lives and what we have done wrong—the good we have done as well as the bad.

"How do I know what is right and wrong?" Doc asked.

D.B. repeated something that he had told Doc earlier:

"You will know because your Higher Power gave you an intellect, a conscience, and an intuition. Your Higher Power will reveal more and more to you as time goes on, yet no more than you are willing to handle. The more you get real with yourself, the more the sunlight of the spirit will come to you. When you are in doubt about what is right and wrong, don't rush; take a few moments to pause, breathe, and become quiet. Your intuition and conscience will open up and tell you. And you can also discuss this with your sponsor or another trusted advisor."

"People who are on a spiritual journey always seek out help from others to ensure they are on the right path. It is not only alcoholics who seek to justify and defend their actions. While it is not only alcoholics who are in denial and are dishonest, denial is a key component to the disease of alcoholism. It is especially important for alcoholics to be honest with themselves, about what they did that was right and what was wrong. That is because alcoholics are unable to distinguish fantasy from truth. Faith without work is dead."

"Step Four involves work because it requires courage for you to search yourself, your motives, and your actions. We alcoholics like to blame everyone else for our problems. We blame our mothers and fathers, our sisters and brothers, our aunts and uncles, our friends, our spouses, our partners, our colleagues, and our bosses. Sure, other people can be wrong and they frequently are, but when doing Step Four, you are searching yourself, not others. You are examining your part in the situation, not theirs. I know it is hard. When you point one finger at others, four fingers are pointing back at you. But we don't like to look at those four fingers pointing back."

"The good news, Doc, is that you can do it. Courage is facing your fear and shining a flashlight on your own personality, your soul, your "I Am." Something really great is going to come out of this. You are going to discover yourself for the first time. As it says on page 64 of The Big Book, our drinking alcohol in excess was but a symptom of the problem and we have to get down to causes and conditions.

It says it in black and white in The Big Book that 'we have not been only mentally and physically ill, we have been spiritually sick. When the spiritual malady is overcome, we straighten out mentally and physically (page 64).'"

"Your alcoholic journey was a detour from your spiritual journey. Your alcohol was a form of cheap grace. It was not the real thing, it was the fake thing and was not able to give you lasting pleasure. You are now on your journey for the real thing, a spiritual awakening that requires you to take a moral inventory."

Moral Inventory

As we noted before, a moral inventory is taking stock of what you have done right as well as what was wrong, your assets and your liabilities. In terms of where we were wrong, The Big Book says that we need to identify situations where we are selfish, dishonest, and inconsiderate. On page 69 of The Big Book, the following is written:

"We subjected each relation to this test – was it selfish or not?"

In terms of assets, this means that you look at where you have made a positive difference for yourself and others.

The Fourth Step

The Big Book suggests that we do a fourth step by writing. You don't have to but like everything else in the Twelve Steps, it is strongly suggested. In the Foreword to the first edition of The Big Book, and referenced in every subsequent edition there is the sentence: "To show alcoholics precisely how we have recovered." While the two of us do not know why the last five words were italicized, we gather it is because of the importance of doing the steps in the order they were written along with the guidelines suggested.

Writing your inventory will ensure that your mind doesn't try to run away and evade the issues. You will see your situation in black and white, which will help you better gain a perspective, and be able to see things clearer. Alcoholics tend to think in extremes. They are either overly puffed-up with pride, thinking they are better than everyone else, or they are filled with shame and remorse, believing they are worse than anyone else. Alcoholics lack perspective. When working the fourth step, you gain a more accurate picture of yourself.

The Big Book notes that resentment is the biggest problem for alcoholics.

Resentment is a highly-charged negative emotion that causes destruction to your mind, heart, and soul. As D.B. says, "It is as simple as that." The Big Book notes that all forms of spiritual disease follow resentment. Resentments, burning anger, and the desire for revenge are like taking poison and expecting the other person to die.

The truth is that you die inside. Resentments cause harm to yourself and others. They ruin your chances for peace and serenity. They ruin your life.

It is advisable that you allow yourself time to write your Step Four list. It would be best if you are able to set aside several hours in a place where you have privacy and will not be interrupted. To begin your Step Four, make three columns, as The Big Book suggests. In the first column, make a list of your resentments of people, places, and things. The people can be living or deceased; what matters is that the list is honest and thorough. In the second column, write the cause of the resentment. The cause is why you became resentful. Write out the situation that caused your resentment and why you became resentful. An example is provided on page 65 of The Big Book. In the third column, write how that resentment affected you. Did it affect your self-esteem, your confidence, your finances, or your feelings of safety and security? Be as thorough and honest as you can be.

As difficult as it may seem, it is important for you to disregard what other individuals may have done. As The Big Book notes, the others who wronged you were, perhaps, spiritually sick but this is your inventory and to take your inventory means you are pointing the flashlight at you, not at others. Neither D.B. nor Doc found this to be easy. Their sponsors said that it required courage, but it was worth it.

Doc told D.B. that when he made his list, he discovered he was resentful about his career, his wife, and his family members. Doc saw that he had been burning with rage, and while he previously never made the connection, he could now see that drinking alcohol was a futile attempt to wash away those negative emotions. They always came back full-force but Doc still kept drinking. He could not stop the drinking and he could not stop the resentments. Both got worse.

D.B. said that was what The Big Book taught him and as a result of doing Step Four he saw that his life, as well as any life filled with resentments, would result in unhappiness.

D.B. said the following: "No matter how hard you try to get those resentments out of your head, heart, and soul, you can't. The more you fan the flames of those negative emotions, the unhappier you become, and the unhappier you become, the more resentful you become, causing you to descend into a negative spiral more powerful and destructive than the deadliest tornado. At least that is what is was like for me. I could run but I couldn't hide. I was powerless and my life became unmanageable. This is why I had to do Steps One, Two, and Three before doing Step Four. I know that I needed help from a Power greater than myself. I couldn't win no matter what I did. I had to ask God for help."

"After you finish the list and the three columns, go back and look at your part, where you had made mistakes, where you were selfish, self-seeking, and dishonest. Self-seeking means trying to get what you want."

D.B. asked Doc what he saw when he did his list of resentments.

Doc replied he learned that no matter how he tried, he could not get rid of them. He felt the pain of shame for holding onto these resentments for so long, and that he hurt both himself and others.

Doc asked D.B. if he should also write about how he was resentful of himself.

"Sure," D.B. said. "You had better, because if you don't, you will never be able to be free. You will never be able to walk with your head held high. You will never be able to fully laugh. Other people may be able to deal with resentments, but alcoholics simply cannot.

They are poison to your soul."

As The Big Book notes, in addition to resentments it is also necessary to make a list of our fears. When Doc did this, he saw that fear ran his life. Doc was fearful of not getting what he wanted. He was fearful of getting what he didn't want, and afraid of losing what he had.

"I never realized how fearful I really was," Doc told D.B. "I always thought I was confident when deep down I wasn't. Alcohol provided me courage, but it was false courage because it was temporary. When the alcohol wore off, the fear came back. And I also now realize something I didn't know before. I realize that my fears could lead to resentments. So I never really had any peace of mind."

"Doc, you have done a lot of work and I admire your courage.

I want to make sure we take out all the weeds that are preventing you from growing a beautiful garden. That is why I want you to do Step Four in a thorough manner. If you cut corners, your alcoholic self, your addictive self, and your fake self will win the race and cause you to go back out drinking or using drugs. Your fake self is scared to face the truth, but your true self wants the truth and for you to be happy, joyous and free."

"Say the serenity prayer," D.B. said. "Because now you are going to make a list of the seven cardinal sins of sloth, lust, anger, pride, envy, greed, and gluttony. Sloth means laziness; and you know what lust and anger means. My sex conduct and anger has certainly caused me to do wrong things, things that I shouldn't have done but because it is in the past, I cannot change it. Pride means thinking you are better than others. It makes others feel 'less than.' Pride can make you feel that you deserve special treatment and cause you to look down on others. To have envy is to feel jealous that you do not have what others have. It makes you feel terrible inside because it makes you feel inadequate or not good enough. Gluttony is excessive eating or drinking. Again, like fear and resentment, Step Four asks you to examine your conduct in all these areas to see where and how it was selfish, dishonest, self-seeking, and inconsiderate. When you look at your seven cardinal sins and how they caused you to hurt yourself and others, you are taking your moral inventory."

Doc did all the above and told D.B. he saw things he did not want to see or like to see. Doc told D.B. that when he looked at his list, he had feelings of guilt, shame, and remorse.

"Join the club," D.B. said. "You are no longer alone."

This was a small comfort to Doc. He told D.B that he wanted to get rid of these feelings and D.B. said he wanted Doc to make one more list—a list of his assets; things Doc did in his life that were positive and good.

"Remember," D.B. said, "we alcoholics like to go to extremes.

You looked at the negative, your liabilities, but you have assets too. I want you to write these down as well. Just remember that any assets you have are a result of the grace from your Higher Power. It is good to be humble and keep your ego in check. Ego is also an acronym for 'edging God out.' We are going to get a proper perspective on things."

D.B. told Doc that he was now ready to do Step Five: to admit to God, to himself, and to another human being the exact nature of his wrongs. D.B. told Doc that he was winning the race, because he had the courage to win over his fear by doing Step Four.

Questions to Consider

1. What does being searching and fearless mean to you?
2. What does it mean for you to have courage?

3. What does it mean for you to be honest and thorough?
4. What does moral inventory mean to you?

Summary

Step Four is about courage, courage to face your fears, your resentments, and your life. When you do Step Four, you are being courageous to be honest and responsible. You were ruining your life with alcohol and you were not being honest or responsible. Now you are winning over yourself, as D.B likes to say. Step Four requires you to be thorough and fearless. Having done Step Three, you now have a Power greater than yourself to help you have courage. Your Higher Power will help you be courageous and honest, but will not do for you what you can do for yourself. You are the one that has to make the list and do the writing.

As D.B. says, "The choice is yours."

It's Not What You Eat; it's What's Eating You

This chapter corresponds to the fifth step in The Big Book: "Admitted to God, to ourselves, and to another human being the exact nature of our wrongs."

The principle behind Step Five is integrity, which is the honesty and truthfulness of our words and actions. The opposite of integrity is hypocrisy, when what we do does not match what we say, when the inside and outside do not match. When you are operating without integrity, you do not feel whole and complete.

When integrity is missing, we feel broken. D.B. says that when our integrity is out of sorts, it is as if something is eating away at us. Sure, the food that we put into our bodies determines how much energy we have, but just as important is the energy the soul receives. If we are lacking in integrity our souls cannot be happy and free. Step Five is about cleaning out the spiritual garbage of our soul, what is eating us up inside.

"It's as simple as that," D.B. said. However, Doc didn't think it was that simple.

"It's simple," D.B. said, "even though it is not easy. Like all the steps, which require work, Step Five tells us that when we share ourselves fully and honestly with someone we can trust, we will experience a weight being removed from our shoulders. The virus of loneliness will disappear. You will no longer be eaten up from the inside. We get the junk out of our bodies. Our hearts open up, as our minds become quieter, and our souls more restful."

Just as there are physical laws in the universe, there are also spiritual laws. Spiritual laws mean principles. The laws of nature relate to the physical universe. These laws apply to everyone, and like D.B. and Doc, you are no exception. If we are paying proper attention to our eating, sleeping, and physical exercise we are more likely to be physically healthy than if we are careless in these areas.

If we live our lives with integrity and principles, we will live a more useful, contented life. We will no longer feel like we are being eaten up on the inside. We will have spiritual health.

Admitted to God, Ourselves, and to Another Human Being

D.B. said there is no one right or wrong way to do the fifth step.

"You just have to be honest," he said.

Doc again said that he was full of shame, remorse, and guilt.

Doc was afraid that if anyone else knew the truth, it would damage not only his career, but his whole life as well. Doc wondered whether doing Step Five was worth it.

D.B. told Doc that humans are as sick as their secrets and like The Big Book says, alcoholics tend to have a lot of secrets which cause them to live double lives, fake lives.

"That is why our lives become unmanageable," D.B. said.

"Your life will always be unmanageable to some degree if you live dishonestly, without integrity. I have learned to become allergic to dishonesty. If I don't, I will slip and go back and have another drink, and for me, a drink would be death, physically and spiritually. Step Five is a sacred step, Doc."

"Why do I have to admit it to anyone else, D.B.? I have already admitted it to myself. Why do I have to admit this to you? And since I already admitted this to myself, what does this mean that I admit it to God? What if I don't believe in God?"

"Remember, Doc, it is the God of your understanding. Everyone has a God or a Higher Power of their own understanding.

As you will remember from Step Three, you made a decision to turn your will and your life over to the God of your understanding, not my understanding. We cannot go forward and do the next step until it is clear that you have done all the previous steps. These steps are meant to be done in order. There are no shortcuts. This program is not about the easier, softer way. You have got to be brutally honest, Doc. I know you can do it, but it is more important for you believe that you can do it. Do we need to go back to any of the steps?"

Doc became quiet. He had never meditated or prayed, but as he reflected on the work he did in the first four steps, he honestly felt that he was ready. He knew that he was ready because he felt it intuitively. He was filled with shame, remorse, and guilt as he looked as his Step Four, and those feelings were not good. He didn't feel good, but he felt right about facing the truth. There was some power greater than himself, his own Higher Power telling him to move forward, to have courage, that there would be victory. Doc couldn't explain this, but he knew he would move on to do Step Five.

"Why do I have to admit my Step Four list to the God of my understanding?" Doc asked.

D.B. explained that when Doc did his Step Four, as long as he did it thoroughly and honestly, he was admitting things to himself.

"To admit it to the God of your understanding, your Higher Power, means that you are recognizing that there is another will besides your own. It is the will of your Higher Power. Admitting your Step Four to your Higher Power means that you are getting outside your head and going deep into your heart and soul. This is the language of the heart, Doc. Your heart has been disconnected from your mind. To admit Step Four to yourself is to admit it to your own mind. To admit what you wrote in Step Four to God, to your Higher Power, is to open your heart. This will set your soul free."

Doc thought for a moment. He understood this. "But why do I have to admit this to another human being? Why do I have to admit this to you?"

"You don't have to admit anything to me, Doc. If you cannot trust me, then find someone you can trust fully to hold your confidence. You will be sharing your deepest secrets and why you feel shame, remorse, and guilt. You have to be sure that when you do your Step Five, you have 100 percent confidence in the person you share it with. You have to be absolutely sure that the information will not go anywhere and you have to feel that the other person sees that what you are doing is a sacred action, an action that is a step towards freeing your soul."

"Your secrets have forced you to live in isolation, and that means you felt you could never really belong. That is one of the great gifts of this program: that you get to feel you are no longer alone.

You get to feel right inside your own skin and get to feel right with others.

"I remember you telling me that you travelled to many beautiful places in your life, to different towns, cities, and countries, where you saw many beautiful sights and scenes. You told me that you heard others say how beautiful it was and as you listened you could also see the beauty, but unlike others, you only saw the beauty on the outside and didn't feel it on the inside. Happiness is an inside job, Doc. You are missing the greatest treasure of all if you do not see the beauty on the inside, inside yourself and inside others."

"When you see the beauty on the outside and you feel it on the inside, you will be living with integrity. You will be whole and complete. You will feel a new freedom and a new happiness, just like The Big Book says. I wanted this, and I think you want this too. That is what you were really searching for with drugs and alcohol. You already experienced the fake thing, now you are going to get the real thing, and it is not Coca-Cola," D.B. said as he laughed.

Doc was momentarily confused, but he was used to D.B. making all sorts of quick detours. Doc was becoming used to D.B. and what Doc liked to call "Do. Be.Isms."

"Can I trust you, D.B.? Can I really trust you?"

"Doc, you can trust me. This is because this program has given me great gifts, such as the gift of being a man of my word and being loyal. It would be my privilege to hear your Step Five. Besides, I am sure that I will also benefit even though that is not my focus. I will benefit because all I used to think about was myself, and now I want to give something back. I want to be a useful member of society and it would be a gift for me to be able to give something back to you, without expecting anything in return. I used to be a scamp, a liar, and a thief. I did things that were as bad or worse than you did, and I will share these things with you too, if it will help you feel better and know that you are not alone."

Doc took a deep breath. He felt deep love for a member with years of sobriety. She once met Bill W. Doc remembered her saying, "Breathe out fear, and breathe in faith. Breathe out fear and breathe in faith." She had the look of quiet, unshakeable faith as she said this. Doc will never forget the moment when she first said those words. Doc took out his list. D.B. and Doc talked for hours.

Doc saw the exact nature of his wrongs and those core defects of his character that were driving him to do things repeatedly in an addictive manner, even though they hurt him and others. Doc was able to talk about himself openly and honestly. He saw that he could finally talk to someone about his deepest secrets which he previously thought he would have to take to the grave. Doc saw that his life was driven by his self-will running riotous, that he had used his God- given instincts in a way that did, in fact, hurt him and others. Doc saw that he was living his life in isolation and that, as a result, he could never really form a true partnership with another human being. Doc saw that he was always living his life by comparing himself to others, and judging whether he was better than or worse than they were, while never identifying with anyone else. D.B. insisted that Doc also talk about his assets as well as his liabilities, reminding Doc to be kind to himself. Doc sensed that he no longer had to run or hide. He was finally getting some real perspective on his life.

At the end of Step Five, D.B. asked Doc what he felt. Doc smiled and said: "I am no longer alone. And I am beginning to feel that there is beauty on the inside."

The Exact Nature of Our Wrongs

Your wrongs are the exact opposite of the principles of spirituality.

The list of the 12 spiritual principles that correspond to each of the Twelve Steps were listed under Step Two. Wrong conduct is self- centered, self-seeking, dishonest or inconsiderate behaviour. D.B. also reminded Doc that wrong conduct is also being unkind to ourselves. The below list will highlight both the spiritual principles which reflect assets, and their opposite, which reflect liabilities:

	<u>Assets</u>	<u>Liabilities</u>
Step One	Honesty	Dishonesty
Step Two	Hope	Despair
Step Three	Faith	Cynical
Step Four	Courage	Fear
Step Five	Integrity	Dishonesty
Step Six	Willingness	Unwillingness
Step Seven	Humility	Self-Justification
Step Eight	Brotherly and Sisterly Love	Hate
Step Nine	Justice	Injustice
Step Ten	Perseverance	Giving Up
Step Eleven	Spiritual Awareness	Closed Minded
Step Twelve	Service	Selfish

Summary

Step Five is about integrity, about you becoming right with yourself so that you can be right with others. Step five is about gaining a more accurate perspective about who you really are. It is about shedding secrets and coming out of the dark so that you can begin to experience the sunlight of your spirit. It is sharing, for the first time, your real self with another human being so that you do not have to live with fears and resentments. It is about being free from the feeling that you are being eaten up on the inside. Step Five is the beginning of the end of isolation and loneliness and the beginning of feeling whole and complete, of being a real human being, of being comfortable inside your own skin. It is opening the door to the greatest treasure of all: being true to yourself, the real "I Am," and seeing not only the beauty on the outside, but the beauty on the inside, for yourself and others.

As D.B. says, "The choice is yours."

So Little Time, so Much to Love

This chapter corresponds to the sixth step in The Big Book: "Were entirely ready to have God remove all these defects of character."

The principle behind Step Six is willingness. Willingness means being ready. It means opening your mind and saying to yourself that you are ready to look at a situation from a different perspective and act different. You exercised willingness when you stopped drinking, and turned your will over to your Higher Power, and when you did Step Four and made a moral inventory. You showed a willingness to exercise your faith, trust, and courage when you did Step Five and shared yourself fully and honestly with another human being. There is an acronym for how the Twelve Steps work, or more precisely, how you work each of the Twelve Steps. The "how" stands for honesty, open-mindedness and willingness.

As you remember from doing Step One, you weren't able to stop drinking or using drugs until you were willing to do so—until you were ready. Other people may have tried to get you to stop, and it may have seemed insane to others that you kept on drinking even in the midst of negative consequences. The key point is that no one else can tell you when you were ready to stop drinking, just like no one can force you to accept that you are alcoholic. That is something you have to be willing to do yourself.

Everyone has a different bottom when they are ready and willing to stop drinking. For D.B., it was going to jail. For Doc, it was feeling as if he was losing his soul. What was your bottom that caused you to be willing to stop drinking?

There is an old expression that you don't have to go all the way to the bottom floor before you get off the elevator. You just have to be sick and tired of being sick and tired. Some people are driven to become willing to think and act a different way, and have a different life only after they have hit a bottom and caused damage to their own lives, others, or both. It doesn't have to be that way, but for most alcoholics, including Doc and D.B, that is the way it was. They cannot change their past, but they can have a different today, just like you.

"Don't worry," D.B. laughed. "You won't become so open-minded that your brains will fall out. But you have got to be willing to think and do things differently if you want to get different results.

If you keep doing what you have always done, you will keep getting what you have always gotten. And what I kept on getting was more trouble."

"Doc, what I want to get now is peace and serenity. This means I have to replace the negative with the positive, turn defeat into victory, and turn my fears and resentments into love. All the great religions talk about love being the most powerful force. No evil can touch it. There is a way to have love in your life and love for others."

"There is so little time, and so much to love. But you have to be ready and willing to get rid of those character defects, those things that you wrote about in Step Four and shared with me. You will need the help of your Higher Power, because if you could have done this on your own, you would have already done so. Your best thinking got you into the rooms of Alcoholics Anonymous. With the help of your Higher Power, along with your readiness and willingness to ask help from your Higher Power to remove these character defects, you are on your journey to a new freedom and a new happiness. So little time, and so much to love."

Entirely Ready

The phrase "entirely ready" is a strong phrase. It means that you want something very, very much and not just a little bit. To be entirely ready to jump into a pool, for example, means that you are going to do it, whether or not you have doubts, concerns, or worries. Come what may, you have made a decision that you are not just ready to do this, but that you are entirely ready to do so. The word "entirely" means that you are not wishy-washy about this. It means that you have convictions.

It would be foolish to be entirely ready to do something if you knew it would cause you problems, but haven't we alcoholics already been there and done that? Haven't we been entirely ready to go to any length to get our alcohol and drugs without thinking about the possible negative consequences? Haven't we been entirely ready to continue drinking even when we knew it was going to lead to trouble, but we did it anyway?

What an insane way we have lived. Now that we are on a different footing, now that we have begun to gain a perspective on ourselves, and now that we have a Higher Power in our lives who is going to be the director of the show and lead us into a better life— better than the one we could have imagined—we are ready to do the work of asking our Higher Power to do for us what we cannot do for ourselves. Step Six is about being entirely ready to have our character defects removed.

Character Defects

"Doc, are you entirely ready to have your character defects removed?"

"Just go over with me again, D.B. what you mean by character defects."

"Character defects are the opposite of the Twelve Step principles. You can substitute other words for character defects, such as personality problems, shortcomings, or index of maladjustments if you would like. The English language is rich but when you keep it simple, they all mean the same thing. Your fears, resentments, and your pride have caused torment for you and others. In Step Four, you saw your part in your life, how you were responsible for getting the ball rolling. All the seven cardinal sins are character defects, and like The Big Book says, character defects are your natural instincts that have run amok. Character defects are all those parts of your self-will that have run riotous."

"You need your instincts for survival. Your instincts have given you energy and focused your mind to get a job, start a family, and be a contributing member of society. In moderation and balance, these God-given instincts are good because they allow you to make plans for your life and give you the motivation to get up in the morning in order to make something of your life. Taken to extremes, these good instincts become bad; they drive you to think and act in a way that causes you and others to know no peace, no serenity, and no joy. You told me all about that when you shared your Step Five."

"You used the word 'sin,' D.B. To me that word means evil and that I will be punished and that there is no forgiveness."

"Doc, sin is any form of wrong. It is like someone shooting an arrow towards a bull's-eye and the arrow goes off in another direction. Sin is movement away from good. People use the word in many different ways."

"There is evil in the world, and you had the courage to look at it and admit those areas in your life where you did wrong. The disease of alcoholism is powerful and causes people to do things they later regret. More than two-thirds of the people in prisons are there because of something related to drugs and alcohol. No one is perfect, Doc. You have sinned but that just means you went off the path that your Higher Power planned for you."

"If you do not like the word sin, then use the word mistake. The path that your Higher Power has for you is the opposite of mistakes and sin, and your Higher Power will take you on the path, and walk with you on that path. That is what is meant by turning your will over to your Higher Power."

"All the great religions talk of the power of forgiveness and of a loving God. Our program is spiritual, not religious, which means that anyone can choose a Higher Power of his or her own understanding if that helps to have a spiritual awakening. Remember that a spiritual awakening is that which causes you to see and act differently, to be on a different footing, to have peace and happiness, and to have love in your heart even when things are not going the way you want. To get this experience, like The Big Book says, you have to be willing to go to any length to achieve it. This means that you are willing to do the steps to the best of your ability."

"Don't get hung up or focus on the word sin. Just like when you learned to ride a motorcycle, I remember you telling me that it was interesting how the bike seemed to go in the direction that you were looking. It's the same way in life. If you focus on sin (which is the opposite of good, orderly direction), you will move in that direction.

If you focus on your peace of mind, being kind to yourself and others, and doing service for others, you will move in that direction."

"Your Higher Power can and will forgive you, because it is a loving power. You have to have faith that it is a loving power, so that you can connect to love. Besides, if you cannot forgive yourself, you will never be able to forgive others. And if you don't forgive others, the promises of the program will never be yours. But the promises will be yours, Doc, because you are trying. Like The Big Book says, when it comes to spiritual matters, it is progress, not perfection."

"I guarantee it works. I have seen it in others and I have a seen a change in you, even if you cannot see it. And isn't it great when you see that change in others? You have seen it too. I remember you telling me after one meeting that Erin didn't seem like the same person. Her constant scowl was replaced by a beaming smile, and she seemed less like an adolescent and more like a mature woman who was filled with love and gratitude. She had the help of her Higher Power, and I am sure the help of her sponsor and others in the room.

She sure went to a lot of meetings and did service for others. It happens for everyone who works the program."

D.B. paused, thought a bit, and said that his Higher Power has been good to him.

"You can't take a two-tonne rock out of the ground by yourself, Doc. It is embedded in there pretty good. Think of your character defects as habits that have become so entrenched and embedded in your life that only some power greater than yourself can help you remove them. To be entirely ready to have your Higher Power remove all these defects of character is what separates the girls from the women, and the boys from the men. No one does this perfectly and no one does this in a day. It is a lifetime journey. Enjoy yourself while you are on it. Be kind to yourself and try to laugh a little more.

Don't take yourself so seriously. No one else does, so why should you?"

Doc didn't laugh along with D.B. Instead, he made a mental note that he had more work to do.

Removal of Defects of Character

"Keep it simple, Doc. All this step requires is that you develop a willingness, an entire willingness. You drank for a long time and had 'stinking thinking' for a long time. 'Stinking thinking' is negative, unhealthy thinking. Your 'stinking thinking' stemmed from being so self-centered, so fearful, so resentful, that you couldn't see the forest for the trees. This step does use the word 'all,' but like I said, it is a lifelong journey, so let's start with one of your character defects.

Which one would you like to start with?"

"Envy," Doc said. "I am entirely ready to have this character defect removed. I really can see that envy does not allow me to identify with other people. It always causes me to compare myself, either negatively or positively, with others. When I envy others, I feel as if others are better than me, or have something that I want and do not have. When I envy others, I cannot feel good for what they have, or what they have achieved or accomplished. When I feel this way, and I talk to the other person, I feel confused, upset and anxious. I feel restless, irritable, and discontented. I want to feel good inside, and to be able to extend this goodness to them, but I just don't know how, I just can't."

"Good," D.B. said. "You have the gift of desperation. I bet you never thought of desperation as a gift. I told you that when you started the steps you would learn more and more. You normally think of desperation as a negative thing, but it can also be positive. In this case, it is a gift because you may not have been entirely willing to have the character defect of envy removed until you became desperate. Now that you really see the destructive power of envy, and how it prevents you from being free and happy, you are ready to have this virus removed."

"I can hear from your speaking, Doc, that you are entirely ready on this one. Like I said, people do not change until they see and are willing to admit the consequences of their behavior. When you were drinking, you couldn't even see the consequences of your behavior.

Even when they were negative, you still weren't ready to change. In sobriety, now that you are beginning to think clearly, you can see the consequences of your thinking and behavior. You already paid the price of the consequences of your drinking: misery, isolation from others, and a wasting away of your soul. Although that is a pretty big price to pay, you never had to pay the consequence of losing your job, your driver's license or professional license. You never had to pay the price of losing your family. You never had to pay the price of going to jail. Some people have paid that price, and it is a heavy price to pay. Now you are going to pay a different kind of price if you want to have a character defect removed. You are going to pay now, or you are going to pay later. That is karma, Doc. The price you are now going to pay to have the character defect removed is worth it, and you will be given back a treasure. The price you now have to pay is to give up who you are for the possibility of what you can be."

"You know you are ready to take Step Six when you want a different consequence in your life. Envy may have fueled your fantasies of being better than others, and made you feel inadequate.

You then used that as an excuse to drink or blame your parents. It may have driven you to work harder and harder, but you paid the price of not having a balanced life. You have to be willing to give all these things up, Doc. By giving these things up, by having envy removed from your life, you will be giving up something negative for something else which is much better."

"To have different consequences in your life requires you to think and act differently. Our actions tend to follow our thinking.

The thoughts that we sow on the stage of our minds eventually turn into the behaviors we act out on the stage of life. Be careful what you think about, because it may become true. You cannot plant corn and pick pears. You can't plant negative thoughts and produce positive actions. But I can hear that you are ready to have the weeds of envy removed, and your Higher Power will help you. That is what Step Seven is about and you are ready to go onto Step Seven for the character defect of envy. But remember, you cannot do this on your own. What would it be like for you, Doc, to not have envy? Can you imagine that? What do you think you would feel?"

"I think I would feel joy and peace. I think I would have a lot more energy. I think I would laugh more." D.B. looked at Doc and smiled. At that moment, Doc got a glimpse not only of what was possible, but realized that it was possible. Doc was entirely ready to have his character defect of envy removed.

Questions to Consider

1. What does being ready mean to you?
2. What does entirely ready mean to you?
3. How do you know when you are ready to change? When are you entirely ready?
4. What character defects are you willing to have entirely removed?
5. Can you remove these defects of character yourself, or do you need your Higher Power?

Summary

Step Six is about willingness and being ready, entirely ready, to give up who you are for the possibility of what you might be. Defects of character, shortcomings, and personality maladjustments are all different names for the same thing. They are the clouds that prevent the sunshine from flowing into your life and into the lives of others.

Defects of character are your natural, God-given instincts that have gotten out of control and caused harm to you and others. You need your instincts for survival and to have the energy, motivation, and strength to plan and live your life. Your life is meant to be happy, joyous, and free. Your character defects have caused you to have a fake self, one that could never be happy, joyous, and free. When you are ready to have these defects removed, when you are entirely ready, this means that you sense that there is something better on the horizon and more beautiful for your life. You realize that the time is now, that there is so little time, so much to love.

As D.B. says, "The choice is yours."

You Can't Plant Corn and Pick Pears

This chapter corresponds to the seventh step in The Big Book:

"Humbly asked Him to remove our shortcomings."

The principle behind Step Seven is humility. The essence of humility is gratitude, which is being thankful. Being humble is being thankful for what we have, while also recognizing that what we have in our lives is a result not only of our own efforts, but the efforts of others and of our Higher Power. Humility is recognizing that you cannot do everything on your own and that what you have accomplished has been built on the shoulders of giants. Those giants are the people in your life who have cared for you and about you.

They are your teachers, your co-workers, your colleagues, your boss, your partner, your friends, your parents, and anyone else you can recall.

Without the quality of humility, we would not be able to consider how much we have learned from others, both good and bad. Without humility, we tend to think that we have achieved everything on our own. Without humility, we lack perspective about ourselves and our role in the world. We either think we are superior to others and act like the big shot, or we sink into a morass of self- pity, thinking we are worthless. Either way, we remain disconnected from ourselves and isolated from others. We are trapped in a prison of our own making, desperately trying to get out but not knowing how because we do not have the key.

The key to getting out of the prison of misery is humility.

Humility is accepting that our shortcomings, which we looked at in Step Four, keep us in a prison of our own making. Our fears and resentments, along with our dishonesty and self-centeredness, make up the engine of our own self-will to run amok, causing us to make unreasonable demands on others. This, in turn, causes an upset in others and possibly plants a desire on their part to retaliate. When we make unreasonable expectations of ourselves or others, or when we run our lives as if others are just objects and instruments to attain what we want—although we may get it temporarily—it comes with a price. We are left with feelings of emptiness, anxiety, or anger.

When D.B. says that you cannot plant corn and pick pears, he is referring to the relationship between our thoughts and actions. We cannot plant negative thoughts and expect to harvest positive results.

We cannot sow hatred and reap love. We cannot sow resentment and get peace. We cannot engage in self-centered behaviors that give us what we want at the expense of others and expect to have harmony with either ourselves or others. What we sow, we reap, and when we were drinking alcohol our self-will was out of control. We sowed the negative and what we reaped in return was negative. Now that we are in recovery, we sow the positive to reap the positive.

To get the positive, we have to get rid of the negative, which are our shortcomings. We discovered that try as we might, and no matter how hard we try, we cannot do this by ourselves. We have to ask for help. Sometimes, it seems that no human power alone can provide the solution. Sure, we can listen and learn from others, and share with others, but when we go to sleep at night we are left with ourselves, our thoughts, our feelings, and our shortcomings.

Step Seven is about asking our Higher Power for help removing our shortcomings, with the humble recognition that we cannot do this by ourselves, and that we need a power greater than ourselves for help. Step Seven is about asking and not demanding, realizing that humility means we cannot have everything in our own timeframe, and what and when we want it. Step Seven is about being thankful and grateful for what we have and asking our Higher Power for help so that we can live a life of gratitude.

Shortcomings

As we noted during Step Six, you can substitute other words for shortcomings. Character defects, personality problems, and maladjustments all come down to the same message: they stop us from being able to look in the mirror and liking ourselves.

When The Big Book talks of a new freedom and a new happiness, one of the promises is that we will be able to smile when we look in the mirror and see a smile coming back, a real smile and not a fake one. Both D.B. and Doc felt at one point that they could no longer laugh or smile. That is because their soul, their "I Am" was filled with much shame, guilt, and remorse. When working Steps Four and Five, Doc saw that his fears and resentments—his unwillingness and inability to control his temptations and self-will driven to extremes—caused him to do things that left a negative mark on his soul. That is why he could not look at himself in the mirror.

D.B. again reminded Doc that he was not alone, and that he could also relate to what Doc was saying.

D.B. told Doc of a poem written by the late Peter Dale Winbrow Sr. called, The Man in the Glass. If you are a woman, feel free to substitute your gender in the place of "man." Over the years, both D.B. and Doc have heard this poem at many meetings, and sometimes when it is read by a woman or applied to a woman, they have heard the word "gal" substituted for the word "man."

D.B. told Doc that when we were drinking, our shortcomings ruled our lives, and we cheated ourselves as well as others. This is why we could never be happy. The idea of cheating ourselves and the impact this has had in our lives is captured powerfully in the poem The Man in the Glass (*Dale Wimbrow in 1934 http://www.theguyintheglass. com/gig.htm*).

Doc said: "I've cheated the man in the glass, D.B. I don't like the feeling and I don't want to do this anymore."

"Join the club," D.B. said.

Humbly Asked Our Higher Power D.B. asked Doc to once again review with him the information he talked about in Step Five, about the envy he experienced in his life, and the effect it had on him.

Doc told D.B. that for as long as he could remember, ever since childhood, he was always comparing himself to others. Doc said that he felt pressured by his parents to succeed, although when he was honest, he had to admit this was not the reason he became an alcoholic. "I became an alcoholic, D.B., because I drank too much, and I drank too much because I was not true to myself, not honest with myself. I was too filled with fears and resentments. That is what Step Four taught me."

Doc went on to tell D.B. that while he wanted to celebrate others' achievements, deep down inside, he always felt this pang of envy that he could not really be 100 percent happy for the other person. This was because Doc was feeling inadequate by comparison.

"And what I did, although I did not realize it at the time," Doc went on to note, "was I always tried harder in the hope that I could be better than the other person."

"I wasn't motivated by the desire to be my best. I was not thinking thoughts of gratitude. I was thinking about how I measured up to the other person, whether I was either better than or less than they were. It was never about walking alongside the other person, but instead always walking in front of or behind them. I could never see it from any other perspective. I could never see that others should have been powerful examples for me to be admired, not envied. I could never see a way to identify with others, because I was always comparing. Instead of feeling happiness for them, I felt envy and self-pity, and I always had this gnawing sense of something wrong inside, some emptiness. I now know that what was missing was gratitude and peace of mind."

"As a child, I was always envious of my friend Eddie because he was so smart in math. Instead of being happy for him, and asking him to help me with math, I would try and brag about myself in some other area, or find fault with Eddie in some way. It was always a competition and never fun. Looking back, I remember Eddie being in front of my house or at the park playing basketball. He was playing basketball by himself, and trying to make a shot from behind the backboard, over the backboard and into the net. When he finally made the shot, the first words I called out were that I had made the same shot too. He did not smile. I smiled but it was not a clean smile.

I can forgive myself now, of course, because I was just a kid. But the same pattern followed into my teens and adulthood. Whether it was at the university or in subsequent jobs, I had difficulty getting past my envy or jealousy over the accomplishments or achievements of others. Instead of being genuinely happy for others, I would try to convince myself that I was happy because of what I had achieved, but I couldn't succeed because it was not the truth. Since then, I have learned that if I do not deal with the truth, I do not feel truly right inside."

"Something was missing. I now know what that missing ingredient was. It was the feeling that I could be happy for someone else even if I did not have what they had, or achieved what they achieved. I was always wanting more and afraid that I would not get it, so I never felt like I was being fully aware of what was happening in the present. It was like a cloud of fear that prevented the sunshine from coming in. This fear that not only was I was not good enough but that I would never be good enough, stopped me from feeling good for others. I did not know this then but I know it now. I now know that my shortcoming is not feeling grateful for what I do have, for what I have accomplished and achieved. Instead of feeling grateful, I was feeling fear, self-pity, and envy."

D.B. encouraged Doc to wake up in the morning and make a gratitude list, which is a list of all the things in his life for which he can feel grateful. Doc thought about his health and the fact that he has his arms and his legs, his eyes and ears. D.B. told Doc not to take these for granted because not everybody has this. D.B. reminded Doc that he has a job, a family, and a career.

Doc said, "I'm lucky."

D.B. quickly responded, "No, I've told you this before. You're not lucky, you're fortunate. You are blessed. Your Higher Power has given you a new lease on life. You are no longer a slave to the mental obsession and physical craving of alcohol. You are not chained to others in a paddy wagon and you can wake up in the morning and know what time it is, and what town you are in. Doc, make a list every morning, and put at least 10 things on it that you are grateful for and don't forget to be grateful for being sober."

Doc felt that both he and D.B. had gotten off-track from the initial discussion of envy. On further reflection though, Doc realized that perhaps one of the reasons he could never feel good for others and celebrate their accomplishments was because he did not spend enough time cultivating thoughts and feelings of gratitude.

"Your mind," D.B. said, "is a dangerous neighborhood. You should not go in there alone. Ask your Higher Power to focus on thoughts of gratitude for what you have. Ask your Higher Power for help in taking pleasure in other peoples' accomplishments and achievements and for being able to feel the warm feeling of gratitude, which is a form of love. Gratitude and love are also actions. You are seeking the feeling of peace and serenity on the inside but sometimes you cannot always think your way into right living; you've got to live your way into right thinking."

"One of the best ways you can show gratitude is to do the next right thing, even if you do not always feel like doing it. Make coffee at meetings, or clean up afterwards. Volunteer in your home group in some capacity. You may not initially feel anything, but doing service work helps others, and over time you will come to know yourself as someone who is giving to others, instead of always taking.

You will get outside of yourself, and over time you will find that you do not need others to give you a pat on the back when you do the right thing. It would be better, in fact, if you were to start practicing actions where you are helpful in such a way that others do not even notice. We alcoholics always sought out the parade, and looked for the awards. Now we are looking for a connection to our Higher Power and peace of mind. Gratitude is a feeling and action word."

Doc never thought about gratitude as an action. He liked the idea of not always having to feel his way into acting right. He could act right and allow the right feelings to follow.

D.B. continued. "Know that your Higher Power has a plan for you that is different from that of anyone else, and that feeling envy for others is your will and it takes you away from that plan. You're human, Doc, so it is natural that your old, fake self will sometimes get in the way of your new, true self that is growing. Your self- centered pride may get in the way. In your more difficult moments, when things are not going the way you want, and others seem to be getting more than you, you may find on those days that your feelings of envy are resurfacing. When that happens, ask your Higher Power to remove them. You will find that when you do this, over time your Higher Power will give you different thoughts to think about, and different feelings to feel. You will find yourself thinking more about gratitude which, in turn, will cause your mind to become quiet and allow more peace to flow into your heart."

Doc realized he was able to feel gratitude for what D.B. was saying.

"Remember that your Higher Power will remove your shortcomings on the Higher Power's timeframe, not yours. As weird as it may sound, you may find that you like your shortcomings because they give you a strange sort of satisfaction. Pride at being better than others or giving into feelings of lust can fuel the addictive self; and since those feelings are familiar to us, and part of our disease, they give us a false sense of power, while removing us from feeling balanced and centered by causing us to engage in unprincipled behaviors. This program is a spiritual program, which means we try and focus on principles. Humbly asking your Higher Power for help is surrendering your will to your Higher Power, so that your Higher Power's willpower becomes your will. Then you will find what you have always been looking for: your true self, the true "I Am" that is staring back from you in the mirror. When you find this, you will smile. You will smile a smile of gratitude."

Questions to Consider

1. What are your shortcomings that cause difficulties for you and others?
2. How do you ask your Higher Power for help?
3. What shortcomings stop you from being able to look in the mirror and see a warm smile coming back?
4. How do you show gratitude in your life?

Summary

Step Seven is about being ready, and entirely willing to humbly ask for help. We are asking our Higher Power for help to do for us what we cannot do for ourselves, which is to remove those negative qualities in our character that prevent the sunlight of our spirit to shine. Step Seven is about asking, instead of demanding. There is an old joke about an alcoholic humbly asking for patience, and stating that he wants it now!

Step Seven is about having faith that your Higher Power will remove those fears and resentments that fueled your alcoholism and caused misery for yourself and others. Step Seven is about the principle that what you sow in your mind, you reap on the stage of your life. You cannot plan corn and pick pears. By humbly asking your Higher Power for help, you are making a commitment, one day at a time, to be the person you were meant to be: not your fake self, but your true self. By working Step Seven, you are making a commitment to yourself that you want to look in the mirror, and instead of looking at heartache and tears, see a smile of gratitude.

As D.B. says, "The choice is yours."

Speak Victory, Not Defeat

This chapter corresponds to the eighth step in The Big Book: "Made a list of all persons we had harmed, and became willing to make amends to them all."

The principle behind Step Eight is brotherly and sisterly love.

This type of love is about caring and connecting with others. The disease of alcoholism is one of denial and loneliness. When Doc first came to the rooms of Alcoholics Anonymous, he saw a sign that read "You Are No Longer Alone." Doc did not know what that meant at the time but he immediately felt that he belonged, and that there was something in the rooms which he wanted.

Thinking and feeling need not be divorced from one another but they often are inside alcoholics. The only emotions D.B. and Doc felt when they were drinking were sadness and anger, mostly anger.

D.B. likes to say that Doc is his brother from a different mother.

Doc had to think about that a bit, but he realized that what D.B. was saying is that while it is natural, given the bonds of blood and history, we can feel a special type of love for our immediate family, we also have it within ourselves to potentially connect with everyone as if they were part of a much larger family, the family of humanity.

It is natural for us to bond to some people more than others based on our own temperaments and interests. It is possible to extend a courtesy to others and even allow a deeper sentiment to emerge: that of genuine caring. We cannot fix others and we cannot cure others. We cannot live any other lives besides our own, and it is a form of control when we try to do so but we can at least recognize that others also have their fears and resentments, their trials and tribulations, and their joys and triumphs. We can identify and connect with others as opposed to viewing them as some foreign creatures to be either used or abused.

We don't want to be hurt by others, and we don't want to hurt others. This is what we get to see in sobriety. During our active drinking, however, we didn't give much thought to others, and when we did it was not always the type of thinking that balanced our own needs with that of others. We were self-centered, sometimes to the extreme, and when others were hurt, we either did not notice or we did not care.

Now that we are sober and looking to experience ourselves differently with a new "I Am," and looking to connect with others rather than remaining separate and alone, now that we are ready and wanting to experience the full range of our humanity and emotions, besides only sadness and anger, we take Step Eight.

Step Eight is about making a list of others we have harmed in order to repair our relationships with them. Step Eight is about seeing the harm to ourselves that resulted from our harming others.

Step Eight is about our willingness to make amends in order to rid ourselves of those negative emotions that have stopped us from holding our heads up high and prevented us from us from looking in the mirror.

Now that we are on firm ground, with our roots connected to our Higher Power—who will make sure that we do not fall or fail— we can take the courageous step of making a list of people we have harmed, including ourselves, and be willing to make amends.

To make amends means that you, your "I Am," wants to grow and be a better person. To make amends means that your spirit, your soul, your conscience, and your intuition know what you have done was wrong, and you are now willing to admit this. While you cannot change the past, you can have a different future, starting today.

The purpose of making amends is to get rid of your fake self, in order to become your true self. The purpose of making a list of people you have harmed and become willing to make amends to them all is for you to speak victory, instead of defeat.

Made a List of People We Had Harmed

D.B. asked Doc to make a list of people that he had harmed when he was drinking. Immediately Doc thought of his wife and his two children. D.B. asked Doc to provide a specific instance when he was drinking and how it harmed his family.

Doc thought about the time his younger son was about nine and was playing soccer in a league. Before going to the game, Doc told his son that they were going to the candy store before the game because the store might be closed afterwards. Doc knew this was a lie because the store was open until midnight and the game would finish around 9:00 p.m.

The reason Doc lied was because he secretly wanted to buy some alcohol first, and the liquor store was next to the candy store. When his son went to get candy, Doc went next door to buy his alcohol. He remembered again making a mental note to himself that he would not drink alcohol with his children in the car.

During the soccer game, Doc secretly drank his bottle, and went to the johnny-on-the-spot to avoid being seen. Doc hid the bottle of alcohol in the inside of his jacket, on the right side. At the end of the game, his wife came up to him, asking him if he had been drinking. Wearing his aviator sunglasses and knowing his wife could not see his eyes, Doc lied and told his wife that he was not drinking. His wife then reached out and tapped him on the left side of his chest, where there was also a pocket. Time seemed to move very slowly as she did this. Doc kept silent, knowing that his liquor bottle was hidden on the right side of his jacket. His heart skipped a beat while he waited. His wife never reached over to the right side of his jacket. Through the alcoholic haze, and buzz, Doc remembers thinking to himself: "Okay. This is how a criminal must feel."

To this day, Doc still vividly recalls that thought, and the strange, disturbing sensation that accompanied it. In sobriety, Doc now realizes that the thoughts that came to him while drinking, and his flirtations with these thoughts and others, were a reflection of Doc's spiritual decline.

After watching his wife walk away, Doc looked at an imaginary line on the ground. He walked on it, thinking to himself that since he can walk a straight line, he must be okay to drive. Doc drove home with both of his children in the car. The earlier thought, the one that he had before going to the game, where he stated to himself that he would never drive with his children in the car, did not even enter his mind.

D.B. looked at Doc and said, "What do you think? Do you think you owe anyone an apology, restitution for your wrong, an amend?

Who do you think should be on that list, using that example?"

Doc said his two children.

"Why?" D.B. asked.

"Because I put them in potential danger. By the grace of God, there were no accidents, although I have heard enough stories in the rooms of AA, with my own ears, about people who were not so lucky."

"Who were not so fortunate," D.B. said as he corrected Doc.

"Why else do you think you should put your children on that list?" D.B. asked. Doc was not so sure.

D.B. went on to note that Doc lied several times. He lied to his younger son before he went to the game. He lied to himself that he would not drive with his children in the car, and he lied to his wife at the game. Also, he broke the law.

While Doc was able to convince himself at the time that he was safe to drive, somewhere deeply buried in his conscience, underneath the deceptive cover of the alcoholic haze, he knew that he was over the limit. At the time, however, the alcohol interfered with Doc's ability to think clearly and logically. The combustible mix of alcohol along with Doc's character defect of self-centeredness, drew him into an imaginary world of his own making, isolated and alone, with a false self of invincibility. Doc was living a lie, and he did not even know it when he drove home with his children while under the influence of alcohol.

"You may want to consider putting everyone who was driving on the road at the time on your list as well," D.B. said, "because you also put their lives at risk."

Doc had not thought about that. How was he going to put their names on the list? He did not know who they were?

D.B. said, "Just put the sentence 'everyone who was driving near me at the time while I was driving home drunk with my children in the car.' When you get to Step Nine, you will see how you are able to make amends to them too, even though you don't know who they are. But we are not there yet. Right now, we are on Step Eight, and all it requires is that you make the list."

"Put your own name on the list too, Doc."

"Why?"

"Because you not only hurt others when you lied, you caused damage to yourself too. Lying is a habit, Doc. Like the late Ralph Waldo Emerson said, 'Sow a thought and you reap an action; sow an action and you reap a habit; sow a habit and you reap a character; sow a character, and you reap a destiny.'"

"When you lie, it becomes a habit, and you dig that habit deeper and deeper into the groove of your character. You can wipe a small piece of dirt off your shirt, but if you continue to dirty your shirt with all sorts of grease and grime, it is going to be hard to clean all that stuff off. Like the poem says, your habits create your character, and your habit of lying was part of your false self, your alcoholic character. Now that you are willing to make amends to those people to whom you lied, you are creating for yourself a new character, a new destiny. That's the game you are playing, Doc, a new destiny, a destiny of peace and joy, of abundant living.

"Keep on making that list and remember, don't think about how you are going to make the amends. That is Step Nine. It's best not to rush it and you tend to like to rush things. You tend to be impulsive, and that's what got you into problems while you were drinking, and it can still get you into problems when you are sober. Step Eight says to 'make a list of all persons you have harmed, and became willing to make amends to them all.' The word "all" is used two times in one sentence. Do the best you can, Doc. You're not perfect; no one is, but do your best. This program is a lifelong journey, and your Higher Power will continue to reveal more and more to you as time goes on.

For now, review those situations when you were drinking and list the persons you had harmed. That is a good start."

Willing to Make Amends

As you recall, the essence of Step Six was willingness. Step Eight builds on Step Six and Step Seven by taking your positive character trait of willingness and using it to repair the harm that you caused to others and to yourself. Remember, all Step Eight requires is that you be willing. Other than having a willingness to make the list, and to actually make the list, nothing else is required on this step.

Your willingness to make amends means you are willing to create new thoughts, new habits, a new character, and a new destiny.

You are willing to think, speak, and act different toward those you have harmed.

Questions to Consider

1. What does an amend mean to you?
2. Are you willing to make amends? Why? Why not?
3. What does it mean to harm someone?
4. What does it mean to harm yourself?
5. What does it mean to be willing to make amends to all those you have harmed?

Summary

Step Eight is about brotherly and sisterly love. It is about your willingness to see where, when, and how you harmed others, and yourself, and about being willing to repair the damage. You do not need to know how you are going to make the amends, you only need to decide that you are willing to make them, which is a process of declaring to yourself, to your Higher Power, and another human being that you are on the road to recovery, and on the road to building a new character, and a new destiny free from the torment of a fake self; a destiny that represents freedom to build a new self.

Step Eight is a new journey that takes you out of isolation, misery, and loneliness, to something that money cannot buy. It is a new journey that makes you feel like you belong, that you are right inside your own skin, and that you can have a caring connection with your brothers and sisters from different mothers. When you take Step Eight, you are speaking victory, not defeat.

As D.B. says, "The choice is yours."

The Journey is Long, the Time is Short

This chapter corresponds to Step Nine in The Big Book: "Made direct amends to such people wherever possible, except when to do so would injure them or others."

The principle behind Step Nine is justice. Justice is about righting wrongs. In Step Four, you were courageous and saw how you were responsible for causing upset and harm to others, physically, emotionally, mentally, and spiritually. You saw your part. When you were drinking, you did not know right from wrong, or if you did, the voice of your conscience was silenced by the alcohol. Step Four is about identifying right from wrong. Step Five is admitting and speaking it; Step six is about your willingness to right the wrong.

Step Seven is about asking your Higher Power for help to remove those character defects or shortcomings that would stop you from doing what was right. Step Eight was clearly identifying the people who you were going to approach and admit that you were wrong.

Step Nine is now about action, about actually walking the walk.

The journey may seem long. While it is recommended that you do this step only after you have done all the previous eight, it is also recommended that you do not put it off, because the clock is ticking and as D.B. says, the time is short.

Admitting that you were wrong may cause raw emotions of humiliation to surface, but you are now ready to overcome those feelings because you know that what you are doing is the right thing to do.

Step Nine is about making direct amends to those you have harmed. With every step you take on the way to your destination, you may be feeling nervous or anxious, but you are also strengthened by knowing that what you are doing is right, and that you are bringing justice to your world. You are walking a hero's journey, not with ego but with humility and with your Higher Power.

You are on a journey to right a wrong, to clean your part of the street, to declare with your words and by your actions that you are looking to live a different type of life. You are taking a walk to talk.

It is a different kind of walk and a different kind of talk than you did in the past. You are taking a walk to the past, to create a new today and a better tomorrow. You are taking a walk to a new destination and a new freedom, a walk to give up who you are for the possibility of who you might be.

Made Direct Amends

A direct amend means that you will be both talking to the person you have harmed and acting differently than you did in the past. As previously discussed, to make an amend means that you, your "I Am," wants to grow and be a better person. To make a direct amend means that your spirit, your soul, your conscience, and your intuition know what you have done in the past was wrong. You are willing to admit this by being direct and honest about it. You are going straight to the source, to the person you have hurt in the past.

While you cannot change the past, you can have a different future, starting today.

"What if the person is no longer living," Doc asked, "or if I do not know where the person is and have no way of contacting that person?"

D.B. replied that in the case of someone who is no longer living, a person can write a letter to the deceased person, stating that he or she is an alcoholic and is on the road to recovery with a Twelve Step program.

"In the letter, you describe exactly how you harmed the other person. You start the amend by admitting the reality of your addiction and the problems it has caused. There is no discussion about blaming anyone else. You do not discuss how the other person harmed you.

You can talk about your feelings, your fears and your resentments, your envy and jealousy, and your pride and how these things caused you to be self-centered and hurtful. You are not only asking for forgiveness, you are asking what else you can do to repair the harm.

You are not only saying that you are sorry. You are demonstrating through your speaking that you mean business and that you intend to act differently in the future."

"Making direct amends means that you actually act differently in the future. You can then choose to read that letter to your sponsor if you wish. You may want to go to the gravesite of the person and read the letter there. There are no absolutes; there is not only one right way. What is important is that you are honest and sincere, that you are ready to right the wrong."

"But the person is not there to forgive me," Doc said. "How can I be forgiven if the person is not there to say that he or she forgives me?"

"Doc, it would be great if everyone said they forgave us. But that is not always the case, although in many cases the person will be pleased that we are being responsible. If we are really sincere, sometimes the person does forgive, but like I said, this is not always the case. What is important for you to remember is that your Higher Power will forgive you. What is important for you to also remember is that Step Nine is not about you getting something from another person; it is about giving something."

"It is not about getting forgiveness from the other person, although when this does happen, it feels great. It is about giving. You are giving yourself the gift of becoming a new person, of creating a new you, a new "I Am.'"

"We alcoholics always want others to understand us. I cannot count the number of times that I said I was sorry when I was drinking. I meant it at the time but when I said I was sorry, I did not follow through with a change in my behavior. I would say sorry one day, but on the next day I would continue to drink and cause hurt to someone else. I would yell at my wife one day, say I was sorry and make a promise that it would not happen again, and what happened?

I kept on making the same mistake. I would yell again at her the next day and then several hours later I would apologize. It was an endless negative spiral. Over time, my saying sorry was worthless; it meant nothing. It was only when I stopped drinking and could think clearly, and when I did a Step Nine, that I really meant what I said.

Now my word means something, whereas before it did not. Step Nine is about not just talking the talk, it is about walking the walk.

We cannot change other people, we can only change ourselves, and when you make a direct amend, you are changing yourself, regardless of how the other person responds."

"I want to make an amend to my family about the time I went to a restaurant with them and made a scene," Doc said.

"Tell me again what happened, Doc."

"I had a few drinks before I went out for dinner with my wife and two sons. Actually, I do not remember how many drinks I had that evening. I had become so accustomed to saying 'a few,' it seems that word just flows out of my mouth without me even thinking about it. I do not even remember how we got to the restaurant. It was a Swiss Chalet. I ordered a drink when I sat down. I do remember feeling restless and anxious and I could not even wait for the waiter to give us our menus. I quickly said that I wanted a beer, a large beer. I do not even know if there were different sizes. I just said a large beer. When the beer came, I quickly drank it and asked for another one. I remember our food coming and we were eating. I do not remember anything about the conversation. All I know was I was sitting with my wife and two sons, who at the time were about eight and fourteen. I remember at one point asking the waiter for another drink. He said no, that he would not give me another drink.

I remember smiling, or maybe it was more like a smirk. I pulled my keys out of my pocket, put them on the table, and told the waiter that my wife would drive. I told him that since my wife was going to drive, I wanted another drink. The waiter still refused. I remember thinking to myself that the waiter was being ridiculous, and that he was wrong. Back then I could not see that I was wrong, that the waiter had no control over whether I would or would not take those keys back and actually drive. I could not see back then that he was the one being responsible. I could not see that I was putting the waiter at risk of being liable if I did drink and drive. I asked the waiter several times for another drink, but he refused each time. I remember eating my food in silence. I have a vague memory of the feeling that my children were looking at me, and that it was not a good look, but I did not say anything, I just kept eating. I do not remember how we got home. Now how am I going to make a direct amend for that, D.B.?"

"Doc, people think that Step Nine is just about talking. Like I said, it is also about walking the walk. One of the best ways you can make an amend, which you have already done, is by being sober, one day at a time. Now don't expect to be given a prize or some parade.

But the fact is that you are sober and staying sober means that you can drive safely with your wife and children in the car. Think about it. Your wife does not have to worry about you doing something foolish or dangerous as a result of your drinking. She has trusted you to drive with your children in the car. Your children have trusted you to drive them in the car. And most importantly, you trust yourself to drive sober. I remember you telling me what a good feeling you have inside when your children call you to give them a ride, and you are able to do so. You do not have to say "no" because you are drinking.

You do not have to say "no" because you have a hangover. You do not have to say "no" because you are filled with confusion or anxiety.

Instead you can say "yes" because you are sober. Your family can count on you, and you can count on yourself. That is a living amend, Doc. A living amends is when your actions not only match your words, they speak louder than your words. Do you see the words that are on the police cars in Ontario? They read 'Deeds Speak.'

It means your actions are what matters. You are making a living amends when you do the next right thing and your actions reveal that you are a changed person. Now, when you go out to dinner with your family you are sober, and you are able to remember the details of the conversation. You can focus your attention on others, not just yourself. You are mindful that you are not the center of the universe, and able to perceive what others are saying. Your living amend is listening to others to show that you care. Your living amend is to be part of life rather than a lonely spectator. Your living amend is leaving others with a good feeling, rather than a bad feeling. There was an old-timer, now deceased, whose name was Jack. He used to say that when he was drinking, he would light up a room when he left. One of the gifts of sobriety is that you now get to light up the room when you enter. A living amends is when you shed light rather than bring darkness. I think you are doing pretty good on that, Doc. I see the way your children smile now. You know when you are making a living amend when the people around you start to talk and act differently towards you."

Cause No Harm

D.B. continued: "Some people have stolen money while others have caused damage to others by lying or cheating, whether it be padding expense accounts, taking credit for something for which they did not deserve, or infidelity. The list goes on and on. We have all caused hurt by being inconsiderate or selfish, or through our anger and rage. The old, childhood rhyme that 'sticks and stones may break our bones but names can never hurt us' is simply not true. We can cause tremendous damage with our tongues. We alcoholics leave a trail of destruction. It is best that you speak with your sponsor before making direct amends. This step tells us that we have to act and that we cannot avoid this step. It requires that we be responsible for the consequences of our actions."

"But the step also tells us that we cannot buy our peace at someone else's misfortune. We have to be careful that, when making an amend we don't cause harm to the person to whom we are making the amend, or any others who might be affected. This step requires us to think carefully. We were so impulsive when we were drinking, and we can still be impulsive."

"When we say the serenity prayer, we ask for the wisdom to know the difference between what we can and cannot change. It is a powerful prayer. I am just beginning to have a glimpse of its power.

The key word for me in the serenity prayer when I am doing Step Nine is wisdom. I have to have the wisdom to know that this step is about justice to do the right thing now, not about justifying what I did in the past. I want to be wise and perform acts of consideration and kindness. I do not want to cause harm. I want to show wisdom by getting help and guidance from people that I trust to make sure that when I am doing Step Nine, I am sober, not just abstinent from alcohol, but emotionally sober, without veering to extremes."

Doc then told D.B. about an amend he made to an old buddy named Ely, a friend he had when Doc was in his late teens and early twenties. Doc had not spoken to this person for more than 25 years.

While he did not remember anything specific that he did wrong, it was the general sense that he neglected the relationship because Doc was just too self-centered. He was not there for his friend when his friend needed someone to talk to. Doc was in the relationship solely for what he could get out of it, not what he could put into it. Looking back, Doc realized that he did not even know why his friend one day said to him, "I guess we all live and learn."

Time passed without any contact. But 25 years later, Doc felt that he wanted to reconnect with Ely. Doc wanted him to know that he genuinely and sincerely regrets that as a result of his narrow, self- centered thinking, he missed out on an opportunity for a lifelong friendship.

With the benefit of the internet, Doc was able to locate Ely, who by this time was living in a different country. He was certainly shocked when Doc telephoned. Doc made his amend, again reminding Ely that he wished him well and that he was genuinely sorry that the relationship did not last.

Doc went on to tell D.B. that a year later he met Ely when he came to Ontario. They met for lunch, but it was clear that Ely did not want to restart the friendship. While in Doc's mind there was still an opportunity for a new beginning, this was not what Ely wanted. This hurt Doc.

D.B. said: "That's life, Doc. I am sorry it did not work out the way you wanted. In the past, you may have gone out drinking because you were hurt. Or you might have gone on to develop resentment and then that would have been your excuse to go out drinking. Now, you are doing what normal people do. They experience their feelings without having to run away from them. You cannot change other people. Bless your friend, Ely, and pray that he will be able to have everything in his life that you have in yours. Be thankful for the good times you had with him, and for being able to meet him again, as well as the hug you gave him. Forgive yourself, Doc. You're growing up and it takes time. You aged chronologically but developmentally, there was still a part of you that remained immature. That is what happens when you drink alcohol. With sobriety, we still get to keep a youthful spirit, but we recognize that we are no longer boys and girls; we are now men and women. You're doing well, Doc. As a result of this experience, you will be able to share your story and help someone else."

Questions to Consider

1. What does making a direct amend mean to you?
2. Are you ready to make a direct amend? Why? Why not?
3. How are you going to make a direct amend?
4. Have you discussed how you are going to do this with your sponsor?
5. Have you thought about how to ensure a direct amend will not cause further harm to others?
6. Is there anything stopping you from making a direct amend? What is that?

Summary

Step Nine is about righting a wrong, fixing what you broke and giving back what you took. It is saying you are sorry and this time really meaning it. You are sorry, not just in your words but in your actions.

You are not just talking the talk; you are walking the walk. You are making the amends not to get something, but to give something. By working Step Nine, what you are giving in your own way and to the best of your ability, is justice to the persons you have harmed.

You promise to meet your obligations and then deliver on your vow. Your word now means something, whereas before it did not.

When starting out on a new journey, it may initially seem to be too long. You are wise not to hurry but you are also wise not to delay because time is short. By making an amend, you are reclaiming yourself. You are creating for yourself a new life, a new way of being, a new "I Am." You can keep your old ways or take a journey for something new and better.

As D.B. says, "The choice is yours."

You Can Look Back, but Don't Go Back

This chapter corresponds to Step Ten in the The Big Book: "Continued to take personal inventory and when we were wrong promptly admitted it."

The principle behind Step Ten is perseverance. Perseverance requires power, the power to continue and press on in good times and bad, both when the sun is shining and when it is behind a mask of clouds. How does one persevere when times are tough, or winds of doubt are howling away at our beliefs? How do we stay on the path we have chosen when sometimes life seems to give us detours?

How do we persevere toward our vision of a life of peace, joy, and serenity when life is not going the way we want, or when we feel overwhelmed with problems?

We do this one day at a time. We can look back on our lives but we do not back up and live there. We do not live in the past. We live in today.

Today, we develop new ways of looking at the world, new ways of thinking and acting, and we cultivate new habits. As we mentioned in Step Eight, Ralph Waldo Emerson said, "Sow a thought and you reap an action; sow an action and you reap a habit; sow a habit and you reap a character; sow a character, and you reap a destiny."

The path that we were travelling while active in our addiction to drugs or alcohol was leading us to a destiny of self-destruction.

Before we came in to the rooms, our character was molded by addictive thinking, which caused us to develop addictive habits, which led to an addictive character. Now that we are in recovery, we are committed to thinking differently, and acting differently, while developing new habits to enable us to create a different experience of ourselves, a different character, a different "I Am."

We saw in Step One that we had to surrender because we no longer had the power to fight and win. In Step Two, we began to believe that there was a power greater than ourselves that could help us. In Step Three, we made a decision to surrender our power to this Higher Power of our understanding, and align our will with that of our Higher Power so that life could become a new adventure with greater promise and hope. This meant that we had a new employer, and were no longer the director of our lives.

Our life in recovery is now about letting go of ideas from the past that cause hurt and pain. Our life in recovery is about letting go of the unhealthy habits that led to addictive behavior and replacing them with healthy habits; one of which is to promptly recognize and admit when we have done something wrong.

As the saying goes, Rome was not built in a day. Our past habits have become deeply rooted and embedded in the very fabric of our lives. Step Ten is about examining what we have done right and what we have done wrong on a daily basis.

As we grow in recovery, we can look back on our past as a great teacher, a great lesson, and as a great gift. The reason we now see our past as a gift is because we know that our stories and our past will help others to identify, to feel less isolated and alone. We use the past to remind us of where we have been, as a sort of moral compass of where we were and where we now want to be.

To ensure that we do not slip and go back to a path of destruction, we develop the habit of taking a daily inventory. This means looking at ourselves and the impact we have on others. In Step Ten, we are making a commitment to become more aware, more conscious, and more alert to how we are living our lives, as well as the consequences of our thoughts and actions on both our own souls and that of others. We examine our lives to evaluate and separate what we are doing right from what we are doing wrong. We examine our lives to see what we can change and what we cannot, asking for the wisdom to know the difference. We develop new habits.

We are going to make mistakes because we are human. Old habits may surface, and they often do. That is natural. When they do, and when our old habits cause us to think and act in ways that are the opposite of the vision that we have for ourselves and our lives, when these old habits come back and make us feel restless, irritable, and discontented, we now have the tools for steering our souls, our "I Am" in a different direction, toward the light.

In Step Ten we make a commitment to do what successful people do. Success may be defined and measured differently by different people, but in every case, success is tied to setting goals and using the gifts that we have been given to try and reach those goals.

We commit to take an inventory of our lives to help us reach our goals. We wake up in the morning and ask help from our Higher Power to stay sober, and to help us be aware of right from wrong, so that when we do wrong, we promptly admit this. Then at night, we thank our Higher Power for helping us stay sober. We develop the habit of reflecting on events of the day, what we have done right and what we have done wrong, where we have been grateful and where we have been ungrateful.

To do all this requires discipline and perseverance. It requires power. We get our power now from going to meetings, from our sponsor, from talking to others and doing service. We no longer get our power from the bottle. Most of all we now know we can always call upon our Higher Power to help us create our character, our "I Am."

Personal Inventory

To take a personal inventory is to look at our assets and our liabilities.

The following chart was given to Doc by H., a fellow traveller in the program who taught Doc, through example, how to see the positive side of religion and religious texts. This chart can be used in Step Nine for taking a daily inventory:

Assets	Watch For
Forgiveness	Resentment
Courage	Fear
Self-forgetfulness	Self-Pity
Humility	Self-Justification
Modesty	Self-Tolerance
Self-Evaluation	Self-Condemnation
Honesty	Dishonesty
Patience	Impatience

Love	Hate
Simplicity	False Pride
Trust	Jealousy
Generosity	Envy
Activity	Laziness
Promptness	Procrastination
Straightforwardness	Insincerity
Positive Thinking	Negative Thinking
Moral Thinking	Immoral Thinking
Tolerance	Criticizing
Praise, Don't Blame	Loose Talk and Gossip

You can also add words to this list as you see fit. As The Big Book notes, more and more will be revealed to you in your recovery, and you will discover assets and liabilities in yourself that may not be on this list. The beauty of the program is that you get to be creative in your recovery. You were creative in how you got your drugs and alcohol, and now you get to be creative in a more positive way.

Notice that we mentioned "your inventory." The Big Book reminds us in Step Four that we do not take the inventory of anyone else, although both D.B. and Doc laughed as they talked about how sometimes this was a habit they have difficulty breaking. Each person has to live his or her life, and it is not D.B.'s job, Doc's job, or your job to tell others what to do. We can offer suggestions, advice, and direction to those who are willing to hear what we have to say, but D.B. and Doc have learned the hard way that it is best to be careful and considerate when offering advice. As Doc's sponsor, Les, has said: "Say what you mean but don't say it in a mean way."

One of the big benefits of going to meetings, whether they are open or closed, is that we learn to give people space when they speak. When others speak, we listen; and when we speak, others listen. It is a great experience for the mind, heart, and soul to absorb what others have to say, taking what we need and discarding the rest.

Over the years, D.B. and Doc have discovered they can learn from everyone, absolutely everyone. D.B. reminds Doc to identify, rather than compare, which means to see how Doc is similar to others, not different.

When someone new comes into the program, and we see their despair and hopelessness, we get a chance to reflect on our own journey from despair to hope and realize, with gratitude, that we can now give of ourselves something we previously could not offer: hope.

We get to experience or re-experience gratitude for our sobriety and realize that we can be of service to others.

D.B. said to Doc: "How many grains of sand do you think there are in the world? How many droplets of water are there in the sky? How many stars are there in the universe?"

Doc was puzzled. "What are you talking about, D.B?"

"Doc, the universe shows us that the numbers are so big we cannot even count that high. There is so much on the outside but this just reminds us that there is so much to learn and so many opportunities to grow. When you go to meetings—and there are meetings all over the world—there are endless opportunities to listen and learn from others, while giving back to others. Isn't that what we were always looking for, abundance? Weren't we always looking for abundant living? When I was drinking, I was being brainwashed by the alcohol. Now I go to meetings because my mind still needs a good dry cleaning!" D.B. laughed.

"Seriously Doc, when you go to meetings and share what is going on inside you—the good, the bad, and the ugly—you are giving yourself a chance to take a personal inventory. When you do, you are also giving others a chance to hear something that helps them take their inventory. Just like you eat one meal at a time, one day at a time, you take your inventory one day at a time."

"Over time, you will notice that you are developing more positive habits. When you do make a mistake—and you will—when you do something wrong—and you will—you are now developing the habit to promptly admit this, to both yourself and to others. This new habit means that you do not have to live with the chirping in your brain, what some call the 'yama yama' and others call the 'itty bitty, sh-tty committee.'"

"When we do Step Ten, and promptly admit our mistakes, we are able to rest easier, and are not so troubled, while our minds and souls are more at peace. Step Ten helps us to have peace of mind and serenity, and money cannot buy that, Doc. Happiness and peace of mind are an inside job. When we do something wrong, it stays with us until we get rid of it. And the way we get rid of the negative is by admitting that we did something wrong, to ourselves and to another person. If you are honest, and willing to listen to your intuition and your conscience, you will know when you are wrong. And when you have doubts, you can always speak with your sponsor and others.

There are endless opportunities for learning, Doc. Endless. You cannot count the number."

"So, Doc, what are you learning when you work Step Ten?"

D.B. asked.

The thought quickly came to Doc. He did not have to think hard. He told D.B. that he noticed in the hustle and bustle of life that he is patient when things are going his way, but impatient when things are not going his way.

"D.B., I pray in the morning to be more patient. Maybe I don't pray hard enough, or always really mean it. I do notice that sometimes I can get easily irritated by what others have to say, or if they do not respond as quickly as I would like. The hardest place for me to be patient is at home. Sometimes I feel like I am a hypocrite.

I can extend my hand out to others at meetings, offer a smile, and listen attentively, but when I come home, I do not act the same way, I do sometimes, but not always. Sometimes at work, I feel like I already know what the other person is going to say, so my mind wanders and I just cannot wait for the other person to stop speaking so I can say what I want to say."

"That's good, Doc; you are being honest. That is the foundation of our program. Like The Big Book says, as long as we are rigorously honest anyone can get well and the promises will come true for all of us. Given that you are finding it challenging to be patient, this may help you be more tolerant of others who also have their challenges.

You see how difficult it is for you, so you can imagine it might also be difficult for others."

The Big Book tells us that it is not only alcoholics who are sick and have their challenges. We all do. We are the fortunate ones because the steps are our tools for developing new habits. We develop new habits that strengthen our willingness and ability to be better people, to give meaning and purpose to our lives, to use our strengths for improving our own lives and for contributing to others.

That is why it is suggested to go to meetings regularly and do a daily inventory. We get to develop new habits, which leads to building a new character, which allows for a new destiny."

Questions to Consider

1. What does perseverance mean to you?
2. What does taking a personal inventory mean to you?
3. What is the reason that it is important for you to continue to take a personal inventory?
4. What are some of your assets? What are your liabilities?
5. Do you set aside time for writing a personal inventory? Why or why not?
6. Do you admit when you are wrong? Do you do this promptly? Why or why not?

Summary

Step Ten is about moving forward in our lives, rather than backwards.

We can look back at our lives and learn from the past, without living in the past. The past is a good when we remember when we were powerless over alcohol and our lives had become unmanageable. The disease of alcoholism caused us to have corrupted habits, which in turn created a corrupted character. In sobriety, we build new habits, a new character, and a new destiny. We have chosen to be different, and do different, so that we can have something different.

Step Ten means that we live our lives one day at a time. While we will make mistakes, and while at times it will feel like we are taking two steps backward, our vision remains forward, for victory, not defeat. So we need to press on, and this requires perseverance.

We continue to take our personal inventory on a daily basis and promptly admit our wrongs, to both ourselves and others. We have our Higher Power who is walking this journey with us, and who will never fail us, as Dr. Bob noted on page 181 of The Big Book.

In taking Step Ten, we are creating a new way of thinking, a different way of doing, a spiritual character and a destiny of blessing.

As D.B. says, "The choice is yours."

Time is Not a Commodity; Time is a Gift

This chapter corresponds to Step Eleven in The Big Book: "Sought through prayer and meditation to improve our conscious contact with God as we understood Him, praying only for knowledge of His will for us and the power to carry that out."

The principle behind Step Eleven is spiritual awareness. The term spiritual refers to the principles of the Twelve Steps. The term awareness means your conscious choice to live by these principles.

When we were drinking, our minds and hearts were clouded by the alcoholic haze, preventing us from thinking clearly. This meant that we were not thinking about living by a set of principles. We were not thinking about others, or the consequences of our behaviors; we were not thinking about our Higher Power, or the word spiritual.

When we were drinking, we treated time as if it was a commodity, rather than treating it as a gift.

The reason for this was because we could not really see anything beyond the bottle. We could not see a vision and a purpose for our lives.

To be spiritually aware is to think of time as something precious, a gift. To be spiritually aware is to be thankful for our lives.

It is to have a purpose for our lives and experience gratitude as part of that purpose.

This does not mean life will be easy. We all have good and bad days and circumstances do not always unfold the way we would like.

To live a life of gratitude means to put on a different set of glasses so we can look at life from a different perspective. We can appreciate what we have rather than focus on what we do not have. This is easier said than done, and this is where prayer comes in.

Step Eleven uses the terms meditation and prayer. While there may be various definitions for each of these terms and different ways to go about experiencing them, one simple definition of prayer is calling out to your Higher Power, while meditation is listening to the answer.

You can call out or pray in many ways: through silent reflection, through reading, through song, art, writing, and sports, or through listening to others. You get to choose how you pray, and call out to your Higher Power. When you pray, you are going to that place that is distinctly you, your "I Am." It is this "I Am" calling out to connect with your Higher Power. You can call out in desperation or in joy, knowing that it is the real you, not the fake you.

What is meditation? It is listening and experiencing the answer coming to reach you, your soul, and your "I Am." The answer may come in the form of an intuition, a feeling, or something that touches your conscience, that part of you that feels and knows right from wrong. As The Big Book says, the answers will always come if our house is in order.

When we were drinking, we were controlled by the physical craving and mental obsession of alcohol. We did not have free will.

Now that we are sober, we get to use our free will. Step Eleven is specific in what we are to ask for when we think about how we are going to use our free will. It is about asking for the knowledge of our Higher Power's will for us, so that we can live a true life and not a fake life.

To live a spiritual life by principles means that we get to choose between right and wrong. We are not perfect and we are not saints.

The actions that we take will yield consequences and we will learn from them. Step Eleven tells us that our fake selves may want to move life in one direction, but our Higher Power—calling out from the wilderness to our true selves—wants us to travel a different path, one that will lead to blessing. Being human, we may find ourselves struggling with conflicts and temptations. The clamour of our pressing urges is like noise that prevents us from hearing the answer from our Higher Power. When we do get the answer to our prayers, and hear the knowledge of what our Higher Power wants us to do, we ask for the power to carry that out.

Time is a not a commodity; time is a gift. Step Eleven is about asking our Higher Power for the answer to use that gift wisely. We are asking for the courage to change the things we can, accept the things we cannot change, and the wisdom to know the difference.

Seeking Conscious Contact With
Our Higher Power

As noted in Step Ten, when we take a personal inventory, we are looking at our assets and liabilities. When we pray, which means when we call out to our Higher Power, The Big Book suggests that we are careful not to make any requests for ourselves only, but that we may ask for ourselves if others will be helped. You can call out and pray however you wish.

When Doc asked D.B. how to pray, D.B. said, "Just pray honestly. I like to read from The Big Book. Some people like to read from books by Hazelden, such as Twenty-Four Hours A Day. I know some people say a prayer of thanks and gratitude as soon as they get out of bed, before they do anything else. This helps to remind them to stay in conscious contact with their Higher Power."

"It is so easy to live our lives on autopilot and remain unaware about what we are doing, and how we are doing it. That's what we were doing when we were drinking. Now that we are working the steps, we are making a conscious decision to live our lives fully, not on autopilot, but very much awake."

"The famous British poet, Rudyard Kipling wrote a poem called If. In it, he writes that 'if you can fill the unforgiving minute with sixty seconds worth of distance run,' you will experience something very special. He was talking about making each moment in your life count, every second. He was saying that time is a gift, and not to waste it.

"I wasted a lot of years of my life while I was drinking. Sometimes I did not know if it was morning or evening. I could not tell what time it was and I did not care. All I cared about was the drink. I could not see beyond the bottle. Now, when I wake up in the morning, I thank my Higher

Power for the gift of a new day, a day with purpose. I get to work with others who are still active in their addiction, and while I cannot change others, as long as they are asking for my help, I can pray to my Higher Power to be an example of what is possible in sobriety. And I find that I need to pray, Doc, every morning for the power to carry out my intentions, for the power to stay on course and not be diverted or distracted. Without prayer, I find myself going back and reverting to being selfish and I tend to become more impatient"

"When I pray, I find that time seems to expand and my mind and heart become more still, enabling me to receive the strength to do what I really want to do, and be who I really want to be. When I pray, I pray to remember that even though I am 10 years sober, I am still an alcoholic. I pray to never forget the stories I hear in the rooms about people who go back out drinking and warn us that it only gets worse. When I pray, I ask my Higher Power to never let me forget where I came from so that I do not have to go back to a life of self- centered misery. I pray for my Higher Power to make every second count, so that I can be aware of each of the gifts that are all around me. There are endless opportunities to make use of one's own talents and abilities, and I ask my Higher Power to put people in my path who will keep my eyes open to the possibility. I also ask my Higher Power to help me remain less judgmental, because I have learned that sometimes I have given people advice even when they do not want this, so I have to be careful on that one. Doc, my day goes better if I pray, so I try and do it first thing in the morning before I do anything else. It feels like I have a partner who is with me always and that is a good feeling. And every night I say a prayer of thanks and gratitude."

"How do you know that prayer really works, D.B.? I mean, how do you know that you are not just talking to yourself? I know of some people who are atheists and agnostics who say it is nothing more than that."

"Doc, in The Big Book, on page 14, Bill W. says 'God comes to most men gradually, but His impact on me was sudden and profound.' On page 181, Dr. Bob, says, 'Your Heavenly Father will never let you down.'"

"This is what they said, Doc. Each person has to live his or her life the way he or she chooses. It is not for me to convince anyone.

Remember, Step Eleven says 'God as we understood Him.' Do not, I repeat, do not get hung up on the words 'God' or 'Him'. The Twelve Steps are written the way they are written, and you or anyone else can interpret them however you want. That is the brilliance of the program.

"I cannot convince you or anyone else that my Higher Power exists. It is such a personal experience, but when you experience love, you know it to be true."

"It does feel, D.B., that I do have a Higher Power in my life. It just seems odd, and too much of a coincidence that a thought came to me to be around honest people, and then I found myself driving 50 kilometers to a meeting of Alcoholics Anonymous. At the time, I really did not want to stop drinking and I didn't believe I had a problem with alcohol. My children think that maybe I am just being superstitious, that perhaps it was not really my Higher Power and that maybe, subconsciously, I wanted to go to an AA meeting. But I really did not want to stop drinking, so I really do not think that is true."

"Doc, your children and anyone else can believe what they want to believe, and you can believe what you want to believe. People can only speak about meditation and prayer if they are speaking from experience. It takes an open mind and faith to try and pray, especially when you do not know to whom you are praying. But most people who give it a sincere try find that after a while there is something different in themselves, something stronger and more grounding.

I find that I am more peaceful with prayer, less anxious. For the longest time, I did not believe it would work, but it does, and anyway, I find that it helps me. Besides, prayer helps me to remember that I was on a path to destruction and now I am on a path to my true self."

"Is there a life after death, D.B.?" Doc asked.

D.B. chuckled: "Doc, I do not know, although I believe there is. But why focus on the life hereafter when you have this life now?

The Big Book promises a new freedom and a new happiness on this earth, here in this life. Don't you want that? That is what Step Eleven is about, having a little bit of heaven on earth."

As soon as D.B. said that, Doc realized that he experiences some heaven on earth whenever he goes to meetings and gets to laugh and cry with others, celebrate with others, and learn from others. He feels like he is part of something, that he is no longer alone. Doc thought about the places around the world he has skied, and the inexpressible beauty of skiing in the mountains, and simply the gift of being able to go skiing.

"Not everyone has their eyes, Doc. Not everyone has their arms or their legs. Not everyone has the opportunity. Be grateful for what you have. Make sure you say thanks every night to your Higher Power and to the people who have crossed your path. Everyone teaches you something and don't forget to give back to others so that they too can find their own little bit of heaven on earth."

Where Do You Get Your Power?

The last part of Step Eleven asks us to consider how we are going to exercise our free will. We call out and pray to our Higher Power for guidance and we get some answers. D.B. and Doc's sponsor, Les, have always suggested that Doc consult with them or others before making some big decisions. As The Big Book says, when we are on a spiritual journey, it is best to consult with others who can provide support while also holding us accountable.

When we get answers from our Higher Power, we know something is right when we feel an inner peace, an inner strength, and an inner resolve. Still, just to make sure we are on the right track before we take action on something that is particularly important, or can have lasting consequences, it is good to talk this over with others we trust.

Power is a force and Step Eleven tells us that we require this force to take action. The trees get their power from the sun to make food and oxygen and in turn we get our power from oxygen, sleep, proper food, and exercise. That is, our bodies get this power but where do we get our spiritual power? Where do we get our power to live a spiritual life and do the next right thing?

Each person finds the answer in his or her own way. For a lot of people in the program, going to meetings is a great way to access this power. There is a spiritual power in the rooms. It is hard to explain, just like it is hard to explain to someone how you learned to ride a bicycle. Just like you need to get on a bicycle to know what it feels like to balance yourself, you will need to go to a meeting to experience its spiritual power.

Some people sense this power through their intuition, while others become aware of it through their conscience;

others experience a sixth sense, sort of like a spiritual sensor or GPS. By listening and talking to others, while sharing our problems and successes, as well as our experiences, strength, and hope, it is as if the sails of our spirit catch a new wind.

D.B. offered Doc the following analogy. "Have you ever seen Canadian geese fly in formation, Doc? Pretty impressive, isn't it? As the geese take flight from the shoreline, they lift off squawking and in no particular order. Yet in a matter of seconds, as if on cue, they line up in a perfect V-formation. I do not know how they do it, but there is a big benefit in teamwork."

"A flock of geese flying in formation can move faster and maintain flight longer than any one goose flying alone can. I am always amazed at how these geese do it. They must have their own Higher Power guiding them. The aerodynamic V-formation means that each bird has to work less than if it was flying solo. With teamwork, the geese are able to cover longer distances with much less effort. In this formation, the bird in the lead position will experience greater air resistance and will have to work a little harder than if he was by himself. However, when he gets tired he drops out of position and goes behind into one of the V-position lines, while another bird from behind moves up into the lead position, maintaining the V- formation. Like I said, Doc, I do not know how they do it, but I can hear them squawking."

"It's funny, because sometimes in the room it sounds like there is a lot of squawking going on there too, but somehow I always manage to hear what I need to hear and find the power I need to stay strong. While in the rooms, we get to depend on each other, just like the geese do. We draw on the experience, hope, and strength of others."

141

"I need to stay strong, Doc, to live a spiritual life, and live by spiritual principles. Like you, I am flesh and blood, and sometimes my spirit is weak, and I am led into temptation. The power in the rooms of AA helps my own spirit fly in the right direction that my Higher Power wants me to go, which is to do the next right thing.

That's what you have to remember, to do the next right thing. Pray for guidance, and the answers will come. Your Higher Power will be like the wind in the sails of your soul."

Questions to Consider

1. What does meditation and prayer mean to you?
2. How do you meditate? How do you pray?
3. How do you make conscious contact with your Higher Power?
4. What is your Higher Power's will for you today?
5. Where do you get your power from?

Summary

Step Eleven is about experiencing your "I Am" through a new set of glasses, of prayer and meditation. Prayer is asking for help from your Higher Power and meditation is listening for the answer. You can call out to your Higher Power in any way you want, through reading, reflection, song, art, or writing—any way that speaks to you. The miracle of faith is listening to the call coming back from the wilderness, from your Higher Power, who speaks to everyone in their own unique way. Some people hear the answer through their intuition, others through their conscience, and still others through a sixth sense, a spiritual sense, a quiet sense that sends a message, revealing the difference between what is right from wrong. Now that you are sober, you have a choice; you have free will. You get a new chance at life, and a new chance to make the most out of the gift of time.

As D.B. says, "The choice is yours."

Celebration is Good but Support is Better

This chapter corresponds to Step Twelve in The Big Book: "Having had a spiritual awakening as the result of these steps, we tried to carry this message to alcoholics, and to practice these principles in all our affairs."

The principle behind Step Twelve is service. Service is about giving back to others. It is about giving instead of taking. Service is about making use of our abilities to make a difference in the lives of others. Going to a meeting not only helps your own sobriety; it is also a reminder to others that they are no longer alone. Reaching out your hand to speak and listen to another person is a form of service. Being active in your home group by making coffee, being the librarian, or going to business meetings means that you are being part of something bigger than yourself. You add value to others when you serve. Sponsoring people is service work. There are countless ways to be of service, both inside and outside the rooms.

When we were drinking we did not have time for others, and if and when we did, it came secondary to our primary need for alcohol.

Service is spiritual because it is based on the principle of giving back. In giving back, what we get in return is freedom; freedom from feelings of restlessness, freedom from narrow self-centeredness, and the freedom to live a new way of life.

There is a saying in the rooms that sometimes you cannot think your way to better living, but you can live your way to better thinking. Giving back, and doing service work will help you get outside of yourself. It helps people stay sober.

There is another saying in the rooms that in order to keep it, you have to give it away. The "it" that you are giving away is service.

The "it" that you get to keep is your spiritual way of life, your spiritual awakening.

When D.B. is talking about a spiritual awakening, he is talking about how wonderful it is to celebrate sobriety. When he talks about support, he is emphasizing that in order to keep the gift that we have been given, in order to ensure that celebration is not a one-time event, but something that we get to repeat, we are reminded to do service. That is why D.B. says that celebration is good, but support is better. Support means service. Service is the gift that keeps on giving and the energy that fuels the spiritual awakening.

Spiritual Awakening

The term spiritual experience and spiritual awakening are referenced and described on pages 567-568 of The Big Book. A spiritual experience and awakening is discussed in terms of a personality change that manifests itself in many different forms, resulting in a profound transformation in our reaction to life. In the chapter, "There is a Solution," on page 27 there is a sentence that reads as follows:

"They appear to be in the nature of huge emotional displacements and rearrangements."

The Big Book promises that we will have a spiritual experience or spiritual awakening as a natural consequence of working the first eleven steps. As a result of this spiritual awakening, this shift in perspective, this alteration in consciousness, and new way of seeing the world, we are not only on a different footing, but we are now ready to give back to the world something that we never had: a message of hope, new beginnings, and a promise of a hint of heaven on earth.

The phrase "emotional displacements and rearrangements" conveys a sense of dynamic movement, of a transition from something moving from one state to another, of objects combining to form something new and different.

When two hydrogen atoms combine with an atom of oxygen we know that a new molecule is created: water. Both of these elements on their own are highly explosive, but when you introduce energy, and the right circumstances, the two separate atoms create bonds that form a new creation: water that is necessary for all life.

It is teamwork. The electrons of the atoms of hydrogen and oxygen have undergone displacement and rearrangements. Although we cannot really know for sure, perhaps in their own way these atoms have had their own spiritual experience when they combine to form a new molecule.

The physical world provides clues to the spiritual world. We are all made up of physical matter, of chemicals. Atoms are combined into molecules, which form compounds, which in turn become the basis for all forms of life. Yet somehow, those physical entities give rise to something that is not physical, and that is us, you, the "I Am."

The "I Am" is what makes you, you. It is your soul.

When you work steps One through Eleven, what you are doing is putting energy into your system that enables the atoms of your soul to combine in new ways to create a new "I Am." Just like atoms of hydrogen need the atoms of oxygen to create a new molecule, your soul needs to combine with the energy of your Higher Power to form something new.

This process of alignment, of becoming, of you connecting with your Higher Power, is the spiritual experience.

The chemical reaction of you and your Higher Power, of you working the steps, of you listening and speaking to others, of you doing service work, gives rise to the spiritual awakening, which is a new consciousness. It feels as if you are now looking at the world and experiencing the world from a different perspective, through a new set of glasses.

As The Big Book notes, this process of a spiritual awakening can either come in the form a sudden upheaval, or gradually.

"Tell me about a spiritual awakening that you had, Doc?"

The first thoughts that came to his mind were about how he first came to the rooms of Alcoholics Anonymous.

"I have told you this before, D.B., but it still baffles me that I drove 50 kilometers to my first meeting. All I remember is that a thought came into my mind that I had to be around honest people. I do not know why that thought came to my mind. I was not thinking about honesty or principles, and I definitely was not thinking about spirituality. I was not thinking that I had a problem with alcohol or that I wanted to stop drinking. In spite of all that, the thought of being around honest people came to me out of nowhere and then

I drove. Looking back now, it feels like I was given some grace. So what do you think happened, D.B.?"

"Doc, I am not sure, and I know that I cannot speak for anyone other than myself. My spiritual awakening came gradually over time, as a result of going to a lot of meetings. I really do not know the time or date when it happened, but I eventually realized that my Higher Power was always with me. I just did not know it. It was when I decided to connect with this Higher Power that I had my spiritual awakening. It was then that I experienced the emotional displacement and rearrangement that The Big Book describes."

D.B.'s expression changed. Where before he was serious, he now smiled as he belted out the lyrics of the first stanza of the song by the late Johnny Nash, I Can See Clearly Now:

> "I can see clearly now the rain is gone.
> I can see all obstacles in my way.
> Gone are the clouds that had me blind.
>
> It's going to a bright (bright) bright (bright)
> Sunshinin' day."
> It's going to a bright (bright) bright (bright)
> Sunshinin' day."

"D.B., why wasn't your Higher Power with you when you were drinking?"

"Doc, like I said, my Higher Power was always with me. I just wasn't connecting to it. I was not listening to the voice of my Higher Power when I was drinking. There is a beautiful prose called Footprints, written by the late Mary Stevenson that reminds me that my Higher Power was always with me."

D.B. smiled as he said that he now has a connection with his Higher Power. Now that he can see clearly and has worked the steps, he can live a spiritual life, a life guided by principles.

"I am not sure what happened, Doc, but now I am free. I do not have to drink alcohol. I have a purpose for my life now, to be a contributing member of society. I never used to think or feel that way. That is my spiritual awakening."

"But I still need to go to meetings, Doc, a lot of meetings because this is where I stay connected with my Higher Power. All the people in the room, all of you, help remind me of where I came from and how I now want to live. Just like the geese flying in a V-formation, when I go to the rooms, I fly with all of you and my Higher Power. It is not complicated, Doc. The more I think about it, it is pretty simple, even though it does require work. How about you tell me another spiritual awakening that you have had?"

Doc's thoughts drifted back to a time while in the last stages of his drinking, he felt as if he was losing his soul. He looked at a card that he gave his late mother, Joy, on one of her birthdays. There was a picture of Doc pasted on the card, a picture of Doc when he was five years old.

As Doc was drinking and looking at the picture through the alcoholic haze, he noticed the younger version of himself had a big, warm smile, and the child's eyes seemed to sparkle with life, joy and love. As Doc gazed at the picture, seeking to connect with the child in the picture, he felt a cold chill as he realized that he could no longer feel the sparkle of life that young child had. He could no longer feel joy, and he could no longer laugh. Although that feeling for his two children had never left him, he could barely feel love; as the alcohol did its work, as he was drowning in despair, Doc felt that he was losing his soul.

"D.B., I do not know when it happened because it seemed to happen over time, but there was no single moment. I have been sober for 11 years, one day at a time, but I cannot recall when I realized that my soul was restored, when my spiritual eyes opened and I could see that my Higher Power did for me what I could not do for myself."

"Early on in the program, I felt that I could never be forgiven, but I do feel that I have been forgiven. I cannot recall when the mental obsession to drink went away; all I know is that it was sometime in my first year of sobriety. But it took several years before I actually felt that my soul was restored. I just did not think this—I felt it. I felt as if the hydrogen and oxygen atoms of my soul were no longer alone; they were no longer isolated. It was as if my soul had formed new bonds, a new connection with my Higher Power."

"Today, when I look at the same picture of my five-year—old self, I can connect with that person. I can connect and identify with the sparkle and love that I see in my younger version's eyes."

"In the last stages of my drinking, I could not laugh. Can you imagine what it is like not to be able to laugh? Today I can laugh; a good laugh, a hearty laugh, and a joyous laugh. That is a spiritual awakening."

"I feel as if my soul, my "I Am" has been restored. It feels as if I am experiencing something that is very old and recognizable, and at the same time, something that is new. It feels like I have come home, and I am no longer alone."

"Doc, I recall reading books by the late author Richard Bach.

In one of the books, he writes the following:

'It's good to be a seeker, but sooner or later you have to be a finder.

And then it is well, to give what you have found, a gift into the world, for whoever will accept it.'

"Everyone has a gift to give, Doc, but not everyone knows what it is. You have been given a gift, and you know what it is. In order to keep this gift you have to give it away, which means doing service and practicing the principles of the Twelve Steps in all your affairs."

Practicing These Principles in All Our Affairs

This step refer to principles. While we all have our spiritual experiences and awakenings in our own time and in our own way, what is common to everyone who works the steps is that the promises of The Big Book will come true and bring about a new freedom and happiness. We see the world through a new set of glasses, from a new perspective of good and bad, right and wrong.

No one is a saint. The Twelve Steps are a way of living one day at a time. It is progress rather than perfection. Each person will discover and experience the consequences of his or her actions. One of the messages of The Big Book and the promises is that we will be truer to ourselves.

When we attempt to practice the principles of the Twelve Steps in all our affairs, one of the promises is that we will not only recognize the person in the mirror, but we will smile back with the recognition that we have come home.

"I like to keep it simple, Doc. When Step Twelve says to practice these principles in all our affairs, I think about whether I am preying on people, or whether I am praying for people. When I prey on people, I am doing them harm. When I pray for people, I am thinking about doing good and asking my Higher Power for help."

At one time Doc talked to Simon, an old-timer, who told Doc the following:

1. On a daily basis I remind myself and accept that I am an alcoholic.
2. Do not pick up that first drink.
3. Go to meetings as often as possible. Do something that touches on AA each and every day.
4. Forgive quickly if you are wronged.
5. Say you are sorry as soon as possible if you do harm to others.
6. Help others wherever and whenever possible.
7. Pray often and learn to trust in your Higher Power.

Simon emphasized to Doc that in the final analysis, when all is said and done, what is a central key for him is staying connected with his Higher Power. This is because all he has is a daily reprieve based on his spiritual condition, as stated in The Big Book.

Simon said he keeps it simple. In order to keep his spiritual condition, he needs to stay connected to his Higher Power. In order to stay connected to his Higher Power, he makes it a point to touch on Alcoholics Anonymous every day. He states: "Either go to a meeting if you can, or read something from AA literature, or speak to another member. That way you are connecting with Alcoholics Anonymous every day. This will enhance your connection to your Higher Power. At least that is what I have learned. It works for others and it works for me."

Questions to Consider

1. What does spiritual experience and spiritual awakening mean to you?
2. Describe what others have shared about their spiritual experiences and spiritual awakenings.
3. Describe your own spiritual experiences and spiritual awakenings.
4. What does the principle of service mean to you?
5. What type of service work are you doing?
6. What does it mean to you to practice the principles of the steps in all your affairs?

Summary

Step Twelve is about what we do after we have had a spiritual awakening. It is about doing service, and bringing light into the world instead of darkness. When we first came into the rooms, we lit them up when we walked out. Now we light up the rooms when we walk in. There are countless ways to give back, to give to others, to do service. Going to meetings, taking a role at the meetings and in our home group are great foundational steps. Step Twelve, though, tells us to practice the principles of service in all our affairs, which means outside the rooms of Alcoholics Anonymous as well as on the full stage of human life.

Step Twelve emphasizes that once we have had a spiritual awakening, we can only keep that gift if we give something back.

What we give back is the gift of our sobriety. We share our experience, strength, and hope with others. We share our own message of hope, in our own way, with our reclaimed and restored "I Am." We have a new chance at life, and have been given a new spirit to make choices.

We get to choose between our fake self and our true self. We get to choose between living an alcoholic life and a sober life.

As D.B. says, "The choice is yours."

THE CHOICE IS YOURS

Doc looked at D.B. and was flooded with memories of their journey. The journey continues, and Doc thought it well and good to reflect on how two very different individuals, with seemingly nothing in common somehow came together in the rooms of Alcoholics Anonymous. They discovered each other in the rooms, in a lifeboat that offered safety from emotional, mental, physical, and spiritual death. D.B. and Doc were brought back from the gates ofdeath to life.

Doc looked at D.B. with gratitude. He saw that D.B. and likewise many others were powers of example to show Doc that it was possible to have a spiritual experience, a spiritual awakening.

Doc remembered how angry and belligerent D.B. was when he first came to the rooms, and how Doc did not want to be around that. Doc did not realize at the time that he was equally angry and belligerent, that he had hurt others and himself.

Over time, and after going to many different meetings, Doc began to see D.B. gradually change. He was still D.B. but there was something different in the way he spoke, and in what he was doing and who he was being. Over time, Doc realized that D.B. had something that Doc wanted.

When Doc was drinking, he went to extreme lengths to get the alcohol. Now in sobriety, Doc pursued with equal vigour something he desperately wanted. Doc wanted his soul, his "I Am."

As Doc looked at D.B., he thought about the countless times D.B. stood up at meetings and delivered his one-liners, what Doc calls "Do. Be ISM's." D.B. would emphasize the importance of service, and telling us that while celebration was good, support was better. He regularly reminded all of us that there was a meeting at York Central Hospital, in Room 1152, on Tuesdays. He told us that we were needed and there was not enough support at these meetings.

D.B. would sometimes say this gently; meanwhile, at other times he thundered that there were patients in the hospital who had the disease of alcoholism and needed to have a meeting.

As Doc looked at D.B., he recalled D.B. saying on many occasions that there was so little time, so much to love, that you cannot plant corn and pick pears, that the journey was long, but the time was short, and to speak victory, not defeat.

Doc thought about the two wolves inside him, just like the wolves inside of everyone else. One wolf is good, while the other is bad. One wolf is honest, and the other dishonest. When Doc was drinking he could not stop feeding the bad wolf. Now, in sobriety and with the grace from his Higher Power along with the Twelve Steps and people in the rooms of recovery, like you, Doc obtains the clarity and strength to choose which wolf he is going to feed.

Doc looked at D.B. and realized that he too has a gift to offer, and he understood that everyone does, even though they might not know it.

You have a gift to offer. It is your experience, strength, and hope. Your gift is your true self, not your fake self. When you work the steps, and fully share yourself, you offer a message of hope. The clouds may come and go, and tears of sadness fall, but the smiles will be brighter, the eyes more alive, and the soul will be more true to itself.

Just like you, Doc knows that he can keep the gift of sobriety given to him by his Higher Power, or he can return that gift. In sobriety, we have free will to choose. We can choose to prey on someone, or we can choose to pray for someone.

Doc turned to D.B. and said: "My Higher Power came to me in the form of a thought, a thought to be around honest people. I now know that in finding the rooms of Alcoholics Anonymous, I have been given a gift, a new opportunity, a new vision for my life, and a deep sense that I am no longer alone."

"No matter what, I know that everything will be okay. I do not want to die but when I do, I know that as a result of connecting with my Higher Power and the gift of the Twelve Steps and Alcoholics Anonymous, I have experienced a little bit of heaven on earth."

"I keep going to meetings in order to keep what I have been given, and work with others to pass on the message of hope. I realize that there will be both good and bad days, and that I can always say the serenity prayer to accept the things I cannot change and ask my Higher Power for the courage to change the things I can, and give me the wisdom to know the difference."

Time seemed at once to stand still and expand to infinity as Doc thought about all the meetings he attended and all of those gifts the program promises. He felt immense gratitude to his sponsor, Les, and for the opportunity to work with his current sponsee Mervyn.

Doc felt an inner peace and deep gratitude because he knew his Higher Power did for him what he could not do for himself. He felt whole and complete. He experienced his "I Am."

Just like D.B. and so many others who do their best to work the steps, Doc got to where he was able to experience the treasure of his heart. Today, he knows that he is free. He found his treasure, what he had always been looking for from the bottle. As a result of what he has learned in the meetings, he now knows that he cannot keep this treasure unless he gives it away. All we have is a daily reprieve. Our sobriety is dependent on our spiritual condition, one day at a time.

When Doc came back from this reflection, he said to D.B.,

"Every once in a while, I wonder what it must have felt like for Moses to hear God speak to him from the burning bush. Do you think that I should pray to have this experience, or be content with the way my Higher Power came to me?"

D.B. smiled, tilted his head slightly back and to the right, and laughed as he said: "Doc, the choice is yours."

THE TWELVE STEPS OF ALCOHOLICS ANONYMOUS

1. We admitted we were powerless over alcohol—that our lives had become unmanageable.
2. Came to believe that a Power greater than ourselves could restore us to sanity.
3. Made a decision to turn our will and our lives over to the care of God *as we understood Him.*
4. Made a searching and fearless moral inventory of ourselves.
5. Admitted to God, to ourselves, and to another human being the exact nature of our wrongs.
6. Were entirely ready to have God remove all these defects of character.
7. Humbly asked Him to remove our shortcomings.
8. Made a list of all persons we had harmed, and became willing to make amends to them all.
9. Made direct amends to such people wherever possible, except when to do so would injure them or others.
10. Continued to take personal inventory and when we were wrong promptly admitted it.
11. Sought through prayer and meditation to improve our conscious contact with God *as we understood Him,* praying only for knowledge of His will for us and the power to carry that out.
12. Having had a spiritual awakening as the result of these steps, we tried to carry this message to alcoholics, and to practice these principles in all our affairs.

THE SERENITY PRAYER

God grant me the serenity to accept the things
I cannot change, courage to change the things
I can, and wisdom to know the difference.

– Reinhold Niebuhr (1892-1971)

THE TWELVE TRADITIONS OF ALCOHOLICS ANONYMOUS

1. Our common welfare should come first; personal recovery depends upon A.A. unity.

2. For our group purpose there is but one ultimate authority—a loving God as He may express Himself in our group conscience. Our leaders are but trusted servants; they do not govern.

3. The only requirement for A.A. membership is a desire to stop drinking.

4. Each group should be autonomous except in matters affecting other groups or A.A. as a whole.

5. Each group has but one primary purpose—to carry its message to the alcoholic who still suffers.

6. An A.A. group ought never endorse, finance, or lend the A.A. name to any related facility or outside enterprise, lest problems of money, property, and prestige divert us from our primary purpose.

7. Every A.A. group ought to be fully self-supporting, declining outside contributions.

8. Alcoholics Anonymous should remain forever nonprofessional, but our service centers may employ special workers.

9. A.A., as such, ought never be organized; but we may create service boards or committees directly responsible to those they serve.

10. Alcoholics Anonymous has no opinion on outside issues; hence the A.A. name ought never be drawn into public controversy.

11. 11. Our public relations policy is based on attraction rather than promotion; we need always maintain personal anonymity at the level of press, radio, and films.

12. 12. Anonymity is the spiritual foundation of all our Traditions, ever reminding us to place principles before personalities.
    Copyright @ A.A. World Services, Inc.

Notes:

162